Doris Charest

STARTING AN ART BUSINESS FOR BEGINNERS

-A WORKBOOK - VERSION #2

STARTING AN ART BUSINESS FOR BEGINNERS

A NEW WORKBOOK

-VERSION #2

Selling your art is a key part of being an artist. As your work piles up, you will start to think about how to get it out there.
Not sure how to market your art? No problem! This workbook teaches you how to promote yourself as an artist. It provides you a step-by-step guide and activities to complete that will put you on the right track to selling your art.

PROLOGUE

I recommend you read through everything, then start at the beginning again, working through each section.

This workbook is for beginners and covers only the basics of starting your art business. I hope to save you the time and frustrations I experienced in my journey. Starting on the right foot is a bonus that will jump start your business.

To start an art business, you need four elements. In this section you will decide on a business name, write a statement, write a bio and organize your curriculum vitae (CV).

Once you have these documents in place, you can start developing your business. In this workbook, you will:

Learn about yourself and your art practice.

Choose which part of your art practice you want to promote.

Learn how to write an artist statement.

Learn how to write a biography.

Learn how to write a curriculum vitae.

Learn about websites and choose one to promote your work.

Learn about logos.

Learn about and design your business card.

You will choose a business name and domain name.

Learn about markets and choose one for you.

Learn about goals and choose your own goals.

Learn strategies for developing your goals.

Learn about networking.

Learn about budgeting.

Learn about pricing your work.

Learn about galleries and art fairs.

Learn about having an 'open house'.

Learn about choosing the right fit for your work.

Learn the basics of social media.

Learn about selling online.

You will get tips and advice that will help your business get off to a good start.

Note: This is a workbook for absolute **beginners** or someone who wants a refresher to their art business. I do not claim that this information is perfect for everyone. This is information that I have learned through my own personal experience. If I had known this information, it would have helped me a lot.

My hope is that this workbook gets you started on a long and happy art career. I want to simplify the process for you so that the business side is as much a joy as the art making.

Every step will help you plan and organize your new business. Make sure you take the time needed to make your business a success.

Let's start right now!

Name your business. For example, you can call your art business after your name; Doris Charest Studio or part of you name like Smith Fine Arts or perhaps, a completely different name like Firebird Art Studio.

_____

_____

_____

_____

_____

_____

Add a subtitle. An example would be; _Contemporary Acrylic Painter or Modern Mosaics For Your Home_ or _Hand-made Books For Everyone_. There should be an indication of the work you do. Are you a painter, a sculptor, an installation artist or a one of a kind jewelry maker. The subtitle should tell us something about your skills.

_____

_____

_____

_____

Tell us something about your skills

For example, 'I make one of a kind paintings of the City of St. Albert and area' or 'I create installations that are immersive pubic experiences' or 'I create small sculptures in plaster that show an abstracted view of nature'. Keep your sentence short and to the point.

_____

_____

_____

_____

_____

_____

_____

_____

_____

_____

_____

_____

Why do I need this information?

The main reason is that you need to decide what you are going to market. If you are like most artists, you are multi-skilled. You can paint, sculpt and create installations. However, you are going to promote only one of your skills to start off with.

You will add your business name, subtitle and description to your publicity and use this information as a starting point for your business. You will be better able to talk about your business if you identify exactly what you do. This is valuable information for you to decide. These items are the start of your business plan. Let's get going.

See you in the next chapter.

CHAPTER 1

DISCOVERING WHO YOU ARE AS AN ARTIST

If you are like most artists, you have experimented and you have now settled into a style that is yours - maybe. You will continue to experiment because that is what artists do. However, it is best to market only one type of work - this helps you to build a following in a certain niche and helps customers recognize your style. This

In my life   By Doris Charest

chapter is about discovering what direction to take with the artwork you intend to market.

Many artists work in different styles depending on their mood or medium. Experimenting with different styles is normal for most artists but it can be confusing your audience. For example, the three artworks in the far column are all my work. The top piece is a drawing with watercolour. The middle is silkscreen. The bottom is acrylic paint with a plant print. To the average person, who likely does not have in depth knowledge about art techniques, these do not look like they are created by the same person. To my artist friends, they see the similarities and can tell they are all made by me.

You will be mostly selling to a public audience, not to artists, so you need to pick one 'style' to promote. This is not easy. I have to admit that I still struggle with this, it can sometimes feel restrictive! That means you should pick the style that you love the most.

What do you enjoy creating the most - big bold abstracts or miniature paintings?

_____

_____

_____

_____

_____

_____

_____

_____

_____

What gives you the most pleasure - painting with a big brush or drawings with a bit of colour?

_____

_____

What can you create in a variety of sizes and still like creating the work?

_____

_____

If you had to pick one style, what would it be?

_____

_____

If you had to pick one subject area, what would it be?

_____

_____

Once you answer these questions, move to the next step; writing about your work.

You have now picked a particular style and have chosen a medium to accompany it. This is the beginnings of an artist statement. The artist statement is the core of your whole marketing plan. You need to work on this very carefully and thoughtfully - don't rush it.

Keep in mind that this statement might evolve over time, as you learn more about yourself and your work. Writing things down helps you think about your work with more intention. With practice, writing things down will become easier and easier. Your artist statement is a work in progress that will never stop changing. Your next step is to put your favourite works up on the wall and examine them carefully. Ask yourself the following questions;

What work do I like the most? Why?

_____

_____

_____

_____

_____

_____

_____

_____

_____

_____

_____

_____

_____

What is the link between these works?

_____

_____

_____

_____

_____

_____

_____

_____

_____

_____

_____

What do I like about these works?

_____

_____

_____

_____

_____

_____

_____

_____

_____

_____

Why do I create these works?

_____

_____

_____

_____

_____

_____

_____

_____

_____

_____

_____

What attracts me to the style?

_____

_____

_____

_____

_____

_____

_____

_____

_____

_____

_____

_____

_____

What attracts me to the colours?

_____

_____

_____

_____

_____

_____

_____

Where did I get this idea?

_____

_____

_____

_____

_____

_____

_____

When did this interest start?

_____

_____

_____

_____

_____

_____

_____

_____

Why did I pick this topic?

_____

_____

_____

_____

_____

_____

_____

_____

What in particular interests you in this topic?

_____

_____

_____

_____

_____

_____

_____

How do I create this work?

_____

_____

_____

_____

_____

_____

_____

Why did I pick this medium to create the work?

_____

_____

_____

_____

_____

_____

_____

What makes your art unique?

_____

_____

_____

_____

_____

_____

_____

_____

_____

Is there an event in your life that caused you to have this particular interest?

_____

_____

_____

_____

_____

_____

What emotions or ideas are you trying to convey?

_____

_____

_____

_____

_____

_____

What is it that makes you happy when you create this work? Is it the colour? Is it the subject? Is it the process of layering paint? Is it.....?

_____

_____

_____

_____

_____

_____

_____

Now you have a lot of information about what you do and why you do it. This is perfect for starting your artist statement. Look at each section and number them from most important to least important. Start at # 1 for most important to #14 for least important.

Don't think about what others might think is important or interesting. Keep in mind that for your artist statement of be authentic, it has to truly reflect what is important to you. Do this now before you go on to the next section.

Putting it all together

The idea is not to write a novel, but to write something meaningful to you and interesting to the public. The statement does not have to be long, two to four paragraphs are more than enough. Depending on how it is being used, the statement may need to fluctuate between the two to four paragraph length. I will explain more about this later.

Here are some examples:

Stories

Capturing memories in a way that a camera cannot, my paintings invite you to explore the subject; quietly discovering what is really there. Each painting is a story waiting to happen. The viewer quietly discovers what is really at the heart of each piece. Within this space I reveal a part of myself and I hope to establish a soul connection with everyone who explores my work.

Some stories speak freely while others require some excavation. Growing up in Alberta, in a large farm family full of personalities, I have captured memories. The subjects are people that were part of my life. My paintings invite you to explore the subject; quietly discovering what is really there. The series of paintings speaks to how people view their interior world as compared to their exterior lives. I paint the dreams or failed dreams. Exposed feelings are the result.

OR:

Views

I love the vistas that show how vast and varied our landscape is. This series is based on the concept of how unique our landscape is and how small we are in comparison to nature. The landscape and my memory of what I saw is the subject matter of this series. By working intuitively I aim at capturing the essence of my memory. My subjects are a blend of reality and abstraction.

Mixed media is my favourite form of painting. My tools include water-based media, ink, and collage. Working in mixed media allows me to re-create the diversity, the essence, and the transformation of nature. I like to experiment with colours and textures. This particular grouping is an exploration of graphite powder. They provide me the opportunity to push the boundaries of image making to a more abstract form while still retaining a sense of realism. Whatever works is my motto. Making the piece successful is the goal.

Within each piece is a story that needs to be discovered. The shapes, the colours and the texture each tell part of the story. I like the viewer to slowly discover what the story is.

Or:

I speak through my works. Each one is a journey, a locus traced from one point to another. They are a journey from within my own internal reality into external reality for all to see. My works are interpretations of personal experience. They are expressions of my philosophy of life. Life is relationships and love is a choice. Joy, humour and insight abound in discovering the extraordinary in the ordinary, the unique in the mundane, the absurd in the moment and the transcendent in the immanent.

Nowadays, abstraction interests me. Also, I am exploring with the human figure by producing contemporary genre works. My art is a probing of emotions, perceptions, metaphor, illusion and allusion. Sometimes a short poem, or haiku that I have written accompanies my works. I like pithy, terse creations that can strike an emotional chord or tweak one's mind. Generally, my thematic interests have been eclectic including abstracts in addition to objective works with figures, still life and landscapes.

Your Assignment:

For now, focus on creating two paragraphs. Pick the top five answers to the questions in the previous section and create a statement.

_____

_____

_____

_____

_____

_____

_____

_____

_____

_____

_____

_____

_____

_____

_____

_____

_____

_____

_____

_____

_____

_____

_____

_____

Next, you need to ask a few people to read and edit your work, this can be a family members or friends. Choose people who know nothing about art, and ask them to make comments and correct any grammatical errors. The important part is for them to note down what they don't understand. We artists understand our own lingo but an average person may not. Your statement needs to be accessible to everyone. Remember that your editors' comments are only suggestions and you make the final decisions on the content, only pick out the relevant points. List 3 points that were repeated or multiple readers could not understand.

Don't feel bad about getting this type of feedback. Just use that information to make your statement better.

List 3 points here:

_____

_____

_____

_____

_____

_____

_____

_____

_____

_____

_____

_____

_____

_____

_____

_____

_____

_____

_____

_____

_____

_____

_____

Now, rewrite your statement with these three
points in mind.

_____

_____

_____

_____

_____

_____

_____

_____

_____

_____

Ask yourself these questions:

Is it better? How? What do you like better about it now?

_____

_____

_____

You are free to repeat this process and ask others to read it again. Pick different readers. Your first readers will be looking to see if you added their ideas. This happened to me in the past.

If you are happy with your statement, let's move on to the next section.

■■

CHAPTER 2

ALL ABOUT YOU, THE PERSON

Now, you need to create a write-up about yourself. This is called a biography or bio. It is not a resume, but information about you as a person. Some artists talk about their lives and their families while others prefer to talk about their professional persona. In this section, I will give you some ideas on how to get started.

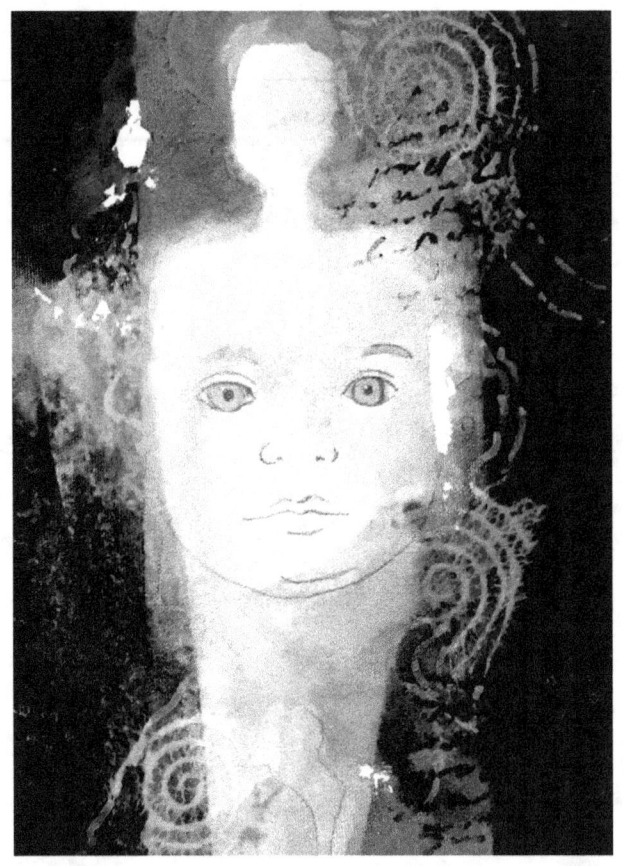

Multiple layers   By Doris Charest

Through your bio, you are telling your audience where you've been and where you want to go as an artist. The best way to get started is to understand your own artistic path. By answering just a few key questions about yourself, you can discover the critical points in your life that have most influenced your journey as an artist.

Most bios are as short as 100 words but can go up to 600 words. You should start by writing a long version, it is easier to shorten something than to add to it.

The traditional biography is written in the third person. However, currently the trend is to write in the first person. I would recommend writing in the first person, it makes the bio feel more personal. Start with I, me, mine, etc.... This is about you. Show that you are proud of what you do.

Exercise #1: Begin by introducing yourself with your name, medium, and background information. This can include where you were born, where you work, and when you first became interested in art. Did you study art? Any instructors that were important in your development? Where are you currently based? Note: Only mention where you were born or grew up if it informs your current work.

Write one paragraph with this information.

_____

_____

_____

_____

_____

_____

_____

_____

_____

_____

_____

_____

_____

_____

_____

_____

_____

_____

Exercise #2 What themes are present in your work? Do you use any unique techniques? What do you want to convey or 'say' with your work? What is the first thing people say about your work when they see it? Has your art changed? Why? What influenced your art?

Write one paragraph answering these questions.

_____

_____

_____

_____

Exercise #3 What is your goal with your art? Why? What drives you to create what you do?

_____

_____

_____

_____

_____

_____

_____

_____

_____

_____

_____

_____

_____

_____

_____

_____

What are your biggest achievements? A major exhibition? Awards? Partnerships? Sales?

_____

_____

_____

_____

_____

_____

_____

Now it's time to put all your information together. You may have to edit out some of the information, your goal is to have one page at the most. Put all the information onto one page and edit out the weakest points.

Ask yourself the following questions:

Do the words flow? Can I easily read it aloud and without hesitation? With a first draft, usually the answer is no. Take out anything that does not fit or repeats itself. Or, you try can use different words to say the same thing, synonyms are your best friend in this exercise.

What most important? You may not be able to include everything from what you have already written. Pick the most important information to you.

You want to keep the tone positive and leave your reader good feelings towards you. Whatever struggle you had, try bring out the positive ways it has influenced your work.

Keep your tone professional. Remember your goal; to be a professional artist. Use accessible language without 'artsy' jargon. Make sure you have someone check for grammar and spelling. There is nothing more distracting than a spelling error in the middle of a wonderfully crafted text.

Some artists mention other artists that have influenced them. This may be important to you or it may not, include it if it is.

Don't judge your work, just talk about it in simple, concise terms. Make the information clear and easy to read. You want to make yourself sound professional, friendly and accomplished.

An important aspect to note:

Your bio will change because you will change and your work will change. You may want to revisit your bio yearly.

Hints:

Good ways to get ideas for writing your bio are:

1. Visit artist websites online and read their bios. You may need to read a lot of them to ones that resonate with you. Artist bios are hard to write and not all artists take the time to write a professional one.

CHAPTER 3

YOUR CURRICULUM VITAE

Your curriculum vitae (CV) provides a more detailed summary of your experience and skills. This is where you list your education, your shows and your memberships to arts organizations. The CV can also include any publications that you have been mentioned in, radio or tv show you participated in or books you have published and more. Let's start!

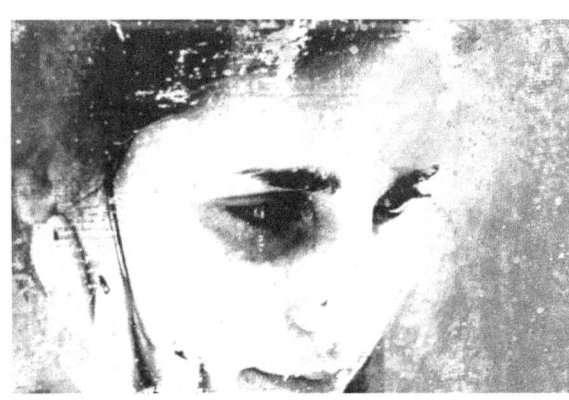

Thinking   By Doris Charest

Part 1. Your personal information.

At the top of your CV put your name, phone number, email and web site.

Leave a space then start the second part.

Part 2. Your Education summary.

This can include your:

-degrees (even if they are not in art) or formal art education such as certificates

-art classes you have taken that influenced your work.

If you are self taught, mention this. Be proud of it! Creating your own path is hard.

Here is an example:

Education

BFA Bachelor of Fine Arts, University of Calgary, Calgary, AB

BED Bachelor of Education, University of Alberta, Edmonton, AB

MED Masters in Visual Art Education, University of Alberta, Edmonton, AB

Part 3. Solo shows.

Solo shows are listed first because they more difficult to achieve. If you don't have any yet, don't include this category. You list them like this:

Date Name of show Name of gallery Location (city) and province or state.

Here is an example:

SOLO EXHIBITIONS

2019   *A walk in the forest*, VASA, Hemingway Centre, St. Albert, AB

2018   *Untouched*, Hub@302, Calgary, AB

2018   *A walk in the forest*, CAVA Gallery, Edmonton, AB

Part 4. Group shows.

Group shows are any shows where you were part of a show with one or more people. This can be things like shows through your local guild, show you had at the library with a friend or a pop-up show at the local market. The format is the same as a solo show.

Date Name of show Name of gallery Location (city) and province or state.

Here is an example;

GROUP EXHIBITIONS

2019 *Winter,* VASA, Hemingway Centre, St. Albert, AB

2019 *Devenir*, Installation & mobiles, Salmon Arm Centre, Salmon Arm, BC

2019 *Devenir*, Installation & mobiles, Stony Plain Multicultural Centre, Stony Plain, AB

Option: Some artists put the title of the exhibition in italics but regular text for the rest. The dates are usually (but not always) in bold.

Part 5. Collections.

Here you list locations where your work was acquired by a group, business or organization. Your neighbour buying your work does not count unless they bought the work for their business or association. This is where you indicate if any groups, businesses or organizations have bought your work. This can be the local realtor, the theatre group that bought your work to give as a prize or any corporate collections. Again, if you don't have any work in collections yet, don't include this in your CV.

You are allowed to say something like 'private collections' in Europe, Australia or Hawaii.

Here is an example:

Canola Association of Alberta

Association Canadienne de l'Éducation Francophone -ACEF

Private Collections in the United States and Europe

Part 6. Bibliography, Publications and Media.

Here you can list prizes and awards you have won, books you are included in and radio or television interviews and any interviews that you have done with the local paper or any magazine. You can also include books that you have been in. Include any brochures or posters that featured your artwork. If there is an internet hyperlink available, include it.

Here is an example:

BIBLIOGRAPHY & MEDIA

2019 Radio-Cité, Artiste en vedette, Edmonton, AB

2017   Radio-Canada- Alberta Le café Show - Entretien, Edmonton, AB

Part 7. Public Art

Here you can include murals, sculptures or any public commissions that you have done. If you do not have any work that fits the category, don't include this section.

Here is an example:

PUBLIC ART

Mural   École Père Lacombe, Edmonton, AB. Design & creation in collaboration with Karen Blanchet.

Mural   Morinville Heritage Association. Design & creation of a historic panel, Morinville, AB

Part 8. Teaching

Include any teaching that you have done, this includes teaching for young people and adults. If you do workshops, list them here.

Here is an example:

TEACHING

2012-2019 Instructor of Art education, Faculty of Education, University of Alberta, AB

2009-Instructor of Art education, Faculté St. Jean, University of Alberta, Edmonton, AB

1996-'Artist in the school', By AFA, Edmonton, St. Albert, Calgary, Red Deer, AB

1995-Centre d'art visuels de l'Alberta- Visual arts for adults and youth, AB

Part 9. Prizes, grants and residences

Here, you list any prizes or grants you have received. If you have done any artist residences, include them as well.

Here is an example:

PRIZES, GRANTS & RESIDENCES

2017 Residence in Caraquet, NB. Representative of Alberta at the Acadian Festival

2011-2013-Creation Residency- organized RAFA at the Banff Centre- Banff, CA

Part 10. Jury positions

If you have juried any art shows, include them here.

Here is an example:

JURY POSITIONS

2015-2019 Art Society of Strathcona, AB

2016 Allied Art Council, Spruce Grove, AB

2010-2018 Alberta Society of Artists, Calgary, AB

Part 11. Profession affiliations and volunteer work.

Include any art related groups that you belong to. If you volunteer for any art group or association, include them here.

Here is an example:

PROFESSIONAL AFFILIATIONS & VOLUNTEER

2000 -Federation of Canadian Artists –Signature

2000 -Alberta Society of Artist-Signature

Note:

You will most likely not use all these categories. Keep in mind that over time, as you spend more time as a professional artist, you will build up your CV to include more and more categories.

A CV should not be longer than two pages, most readers do not usually have the attention span to read more than that. However, if your CV (and accomplishments!) grow longer than two pages, you will then have:

1. A 'master' CV that holds all your information in one spot. This CV is one that you keep for yourself.

2. A shorter CV that you put in your applications for shows and residencies. Using the information in your master CV, you can adapt your short CV according to the demands of the application. For example, some applications will need your teaching experience and not your jurying experience, while others will need your jurying experience and not your professional memberships. You should always include your exhibitions, your education and your awards. The other information can change.

Remember to get someone to read your CV for spelling and grammar once you feel it is complete.

CHAPTER 4

YOUR WEBSITE OR APP

In this section you will make decisions about your website, business cards, logo, and business and domain name. In today's art world, a web presence is a 'must have'. Most people choose to get a website, but some also get an app. You can have someone make a website/app for you or you can make your own. There are a lot of different types of website/app providers, and finding the right fit for your work and budget is the key.

Thoughts XX   By Doris Charest

Choosing a website or app platform:

Step 1. Choosing the right platform for you is difficult, there are so many to chose from! However, it is a good investment of your time and effort because a good website is essential. Before you start, you should have an idea of what your requirements are.

Do you want to have large photos of your work?

Do you want to have galleries or groupings of pages with a theme? For example, landscapes in one section and figures in another or acrylics in one section and sculpture in another.

Do you want to be able to sell online?

Do you want to include videos?

Do you want the website to advertise your other talents? (eg. teaching, paint night sessions, one-on-one tutoring)

What do you want people to notice first?

Do you want to feature your installations or your sculptures?

Do you want to only show one part of your work? (eg. your installations vs your work on paper)

Do you want people to subscribe to your newsletter?

Do you want people to see links to other sites you are on?

_____

_____

_____

_____

_____

There are a lot of items to consider. Make a list of the top items you are looking for in a website here:

1._____

_____

_____

_____

2._____

_____

_____

3._____

_____

_____

4._____

_____

_____

5._____

_____

_____

6._____

_____

_____

Step 2. Once you have decided what you want, you need to start researching different providers. The providers will give you options of the types of templates they have to offer. Browse their templates and decide which one will have all the features you are looking for.

An easy way to find providers is check out what platforms other artists are using. At the bottom of every website, the provider is listed. For example, mine is Artbiz.ca.

There are hundreds of providers so another good way to narrow down the search is to ask friends or people you know what they use.

What you want to ask is:

-Do you have to do all the work of putting your images and information like a CV on the website itself or will the provider do some of the work (for a fee, of course).

-How difficult is it to use this particular template?

-If you have to add or change information, how easy was it to do?

-Is the provider local or does the provider live in another country? If you have problems, you may have difficulty contacting the provider for help or pay extra fees in long distance phone bills.

-What is the annual or monthly fee? Compare to other providers.

-Do you have to pay for upgrades?

-Can you add social media links easily?

-Is it easy to link your site to other group sites that you belong to?

-Does the provider have teaching videos for you to watch to help you put the site together?

Free and not so free websites

By the time you read this, the information below may be out of date. Online platforms change very quickly but this will give you some things to consider

Note: Read the fine print carefully, some sites advertise that they are free but they are only free for a week or two while you try them out. I had this happen to me - I phone up the app provider I was using and asked 'Where is my app?" and they replied that it was deleted because it was only free for a week. What! I almost screamed.

Also, there was no warning that my work was going to be deleted unless I paid the provider to warn me of this. It was buried deep in the fine print, which unfortunately I did not read close enough. Who reads everything through? YOU WILL NOW!

I had spent hours working on this new idea and now it was gone. I was upset and would not resubscribe to this provider if my life depended on it. Don't let this happen to you.

Generally, you get what you pay for. A free website usually doesn't offer upgrades or assistance when you have problems, but good website providers do.

Really good sites offer videos that help you with tutorials on creating your site or even offer some one-on-one time with you. Remember that you will have to pay for any extended types of work by any website provider. They are earning a living too.

Make a list of potential website providers that you are interested in. Beside each one write the things you like about this provider and what you do not like too. You can compare at the end. My advice is to make a short list. This will help you figure out what you like in a website provider. Then do this exercise a second time.

First four website providers you like:

1._____

_____

_____

_____

_____

2._____

_____

_____

_____

_____

3._____

_____

_____

_____

_____

_____

4._____
_____
_____
_____
_____
_____
_____

Decision time. You now need to pick one provider from all the ones you have looked at. Write it down here and list why you have chosen this particular provider.

_____
_____
_____
_____
_____
_____
_____
_____
_____

CHAPTER 5

YOUR LOGO

A logo is a symbol or series of shapes or lines that you create to use as a personal identifier. For example:

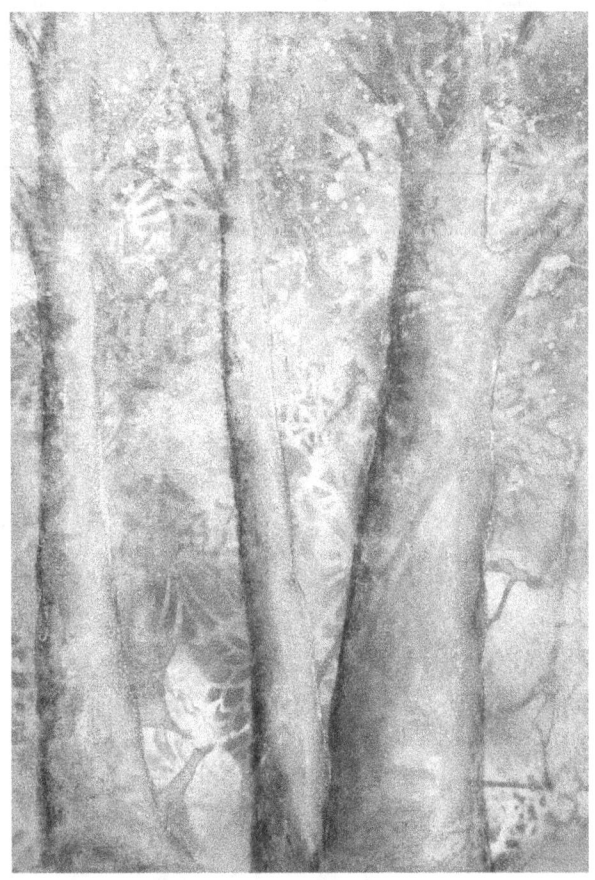

-a circle with a photo of your work
-an artist palette with your colours on it
-a symbol of what you paint (eg. a tree if you do landscape).

Blue Study   By Doris Charest

Choosing a logo

A logo is a symbol or design that people associate with you and your work. Shapes are easily recognizable and they are often used. Common shapes are pots for potters, the shape of your sculptures, flowers if you paint flowers or a needle and thread if you you are a quilter.

For my own logo, I chose a brush making a mark then below it, I added my email. I thought that it was just enough to show that I am a painter.

A logo is very personal. The image or shapes should be linked to your work.

Copying someone's logo is a huge **no**!

dorischarest@gmail.com

My personal logo

You need to carefully craft or design you logo:

1. Keep the design simple.

2. Make the logo unique and easy to identify.

3. Use the same colours as your website or blog.

4. Use this logo on your website, blog, business cards or even your labels for your paintings.

Take the time you need to create something special.

List what items you want on your logo.

_____

_____

_____

_____

_____

_____

_____

DRAW YOUR LOGO HERE:

CHAPTER 6

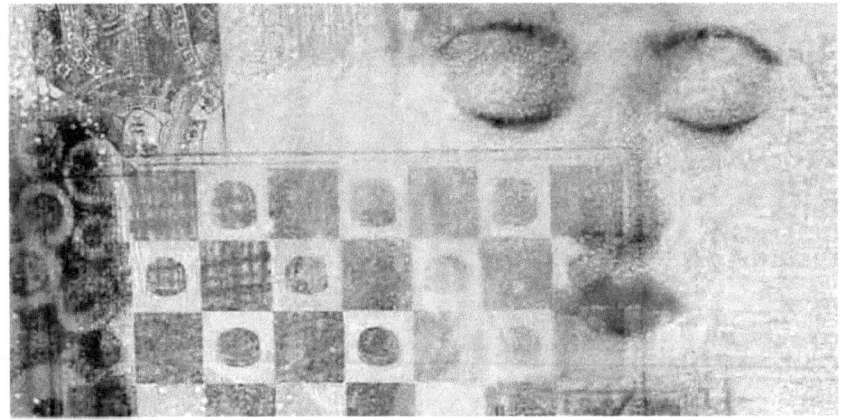

Thoughts #1   By Doris Charest

BUSINESS CARDS

Business cards are less important than they used to be, but keeping a small quantity of them is still useful. You can give them out to people who want to remember your name and look up your website. Give them out whenever you can. You can never tell when someone will look you up.

The information that you put on your business card will allow your future clients to contact you. You want to think about how you want people to remember you. Colours, images and the logo are all 'name recognition' elements that you should choose carefully.

What you absolutely need on your business card:

● Your name.

● Your email -so that they can contact you.

● Your website -so they can look up your work.

● Your logo.

● Optional: an image that represents you.

Do not put:

- Your street address.

- Your personal phone number (you can put a business phone number).

- Photos of you or your family or anything personal.

More business card suggestions:

1. You can put a photo of your artwork on your card along with your name, your website and email.

2. You can put your logo on your card with your information.

3. You can put both the logo and an image on your card if there is room.

4. Don't overload your card, keep it simple.

5. Choose the same colours that are on your website or blog. You want the colour scheme to be part of your brand.

Design your business card here:

There are some websites that have business card templates you can start with and modify for your needs:

• Vistaprint

• Moo

• Canva

You can also visit a local designer and ask them to do this work for you.

Another option is to hire someone online to do the work for you. There are listings of people that can do this kind of work on sites like Fivver.com. They are not the only ones. Search for them online and you may be able to get a good deal.

Write your list of possibles here:_____

_____

_____

_____

_____

_____

_____

_____

_____

_____

_____

_____

_____

_____

_____

_____

CHAPTER 7

BUSINESS NAMES AND DOMAIN NAMES

Choosing your business name is difficult. You have lots of ideas but choose one that best represents your work and your brand.
Also think of your customers. If you were them, would you prefer an easy to

Palette photo by D. Charest

remember name or a difficult name? It is better to chose something simple than something complicated.

Business names:

Choosing a business name can take time. Make sure you do your homework to make sure no other business has the name you are interested in. You can Google the name you have in mind to see if someone is already using it. I was surprised to find that my own name was common enough to have others using it, where I live it is an unusual name. A friend of mine chose a name without double checking. The name she chose was also used by another business in a city close by. Sometimes she would receive mail for the other business. She got a lot of mail when they stopped paying their bills. Double checking is crucial.

Check all possible variations on your name as well. Your name with your middle name (if you have one), your last name alone, both first and last name and any variation that you can think of. You can also use a name generator program.

Business name generator suggestions:

https://anadea.info/tools/online-business-name-generator/search

If you can also check this article out:

https://digital.com/blog/best-business-name-generators/

Brainstorm and write all your business name ideas here:

_____

_____

_____

_____

_____

_____

_____

_____

_____

_____

_____

_____

_____

_____

Domain names:

A domain name is a label that identifies a network domain on the internet. You will use this name for your website.

A domain name is a label that identifies a network domain: a distinct group of computers under a central administration or authority. Within the Internet, domain names are formed by the rules and procedures of the Domain Name System (DNS). Any name registered in the DNS is a domain name.

The registration of these domain names is usually administered by domain name registrars who sell their services to the public.

Some registrars include:

- GoDaddy.com

- Namecheap.com

- Bluehost.com

- HostGator.com

- Name.com

There are hundreds of registrars so shop around for the best price. Domain names are usually fairly inexpensive. Consider going for a middle range price. You want to choose a provider that will not go out of business and has a good reputation. Ask your computer savvy friends what they are using.

Write your favourite registrar here:

_____

_____

_____

_____

_____

When using your name, you can write your name as one word. ie. *dorischarest.ca* or you can add a full stop between your first or last name *doris.charest.ca*.

The way you write your business name is up to you, but keeping it simple is the best approach. Here is a review of important points:

1   Make your domain name short and memorable.

2   Make your domain name pronounceable.

3   It should be easy to spell a single way.

4   Don't use hyphens.

Try to create a link between your business name and your domain name so people can easily find you. You can have the same name for both or a small variation on the name. ie. Love Florals as a business name; love.florals or I.love.florals as domain name.

Look at the most popular businesses you know or like. Check out their names and domain names. Are they the same?

Write an example of your possible business names with their domain name possibilities here:

_____

_____

_____

_____

_____

_____

_____

More advice

1. *Think of how you want your customers to remember you.*

2. *A super specific name might not be a good long term. For example, now you are painting flowers and choose something related to flowers. But five years from now, you may not like to paint flowers anymore, then what do you do?*

3. *Name recognition is important. In my own situation, I decided to stick to something very simple: my name!*

4. *People can find my name on my website, my blog, my artwork, my....everything. Make sure you use your business names as much as possible.*

CHAPTER 8

FINDING YOUR MARKET

Thinking of the future By Doris
Charest

Find your Target Market In this section you will figure out the right market for you, analyze the competition, set goals and get organized. There are hundreds of markets 'out there' for you. Finding the right one is important and one of the hardest parts of your job.

Start finding your target market

Keep in mind that you will need to take some bold steps here. You will have to talk to people you do not know.

You will need to have your 'artist statement' done and in your hand, ready to hand out. You will need a website. You will need business cards.

Decide how you want to start. Do you want to approach a gallery? Do you want to participate in an art fair? Do you want to host your own show?

Make a list of your target market (s) here:

_____

_____

_____

_____

_____

_____

_____

_____

_____

_____

_____

_____

_____

The following will help you decide what the appropriate venue for you is. You may even choose more than one venue.

Approaching a gallery

Step 1. Start close to home. Go to your local galleries and shops for fine art, and make a list of what they sell.

When you have seen all the work in every gallery, you need to decide which one might be the best fit for you. Ask yourself:

Does the gallery have subject matter like yours? For example, if the gallery handles mostly abstracts, do you create abstracts that are just a bit different from the ones in the gallery? If that is the case, you may be a fit for the gallery.

If you create realistic landscapes, they will most likely not be drawn to your work. You need to find a gallery that carries realistic landscapes.

Step. 2. When you find a gallery that may be a fit, talk to the manager or owner. Ask them questions like:

Does the gallery take local artists?

Does the gallery take beginner artists?

Who are your best sellers?

What is the gallery looking for? Bright colours? Neutral colours?

To whom does the gallery sell? Designers, walk-in traffic, regular collectors that shop at the gallery, large companies or museums?

Be curious and keep the conversation casual. Let the manager do the talking.

At the end of the conversation, if you feel that you might be a good fit for them, ask them if are they taking on new artists. They will be honest and give you a direct answer. Make it clear that you are looking for someone to represent you. Tell them that you would like to make an appointment with them so they can look at your work. If they ask to see your work now, you can choose to:

1. Have a tablet ready with your images.

2. Have your website ready for them to view.

3. Carry a portfolio with printed images to show them. Most will want to see a website though.

This option is only if you do not have your website ready.

They may say that they are not taking on new artists. If they look at your work, ask them for suggestions. Ask if they know of any gallery that might be a good fit.

Don't be afraid to ask for recommendations. They may know galleries that you have not found yet. Gallery managers are art lovers and they have a lot of knowledge that can help you.

List the top five galleries that you have visited. Beside the name, add the reason they are the top five:

1._____

_____

_____

_____

2._____

_____

_____

_____

3._____

_____

_____

_____

4._____

_____

_____

_____

5._____

_____

_____

_____

Pick the top gallery on your list. Why is the gallery is a fit? Write down three reasons this gallery is the one think is the one for you?

1._____

_____

_____

_____

2._____

_____

_____

_____

3._____

_____

_____

_____

Now, make a list of 10 questions that you will ask the gallery manager. You may or may not ask them all but this way you are prepared for the meeting.

1._____

_____

_____

_____

2._____

_____

_____

_____

3._____

_____

_____

_____

4._____

_____

_____

_____

5._____

_____

_____

_____

6._____

_____

_____

_____

7._____

_____

_____

_____

8._____

_____

_____

_____

9._____

_____

_____

_____

10._____

_____

_____

_____

Your next task is to practice asking these questions in front of the mirror. Many artists are shy so practice makes perfect. This is a great way to learn your questions by heart.

When you are practicing, look at the expressions on your face. You need to practice looking calm and interested. If you look scared to death, practice to feel more at ease. It will get easier as you practice.

Here are some tips to practice:

-Take a deep breath before you start. This gives your voice some depth and your voice will not squeak when you start. This is also a way to relax and ease some of your nerves.

-Practice saying your words slowly and clearly. You might find that you need to change your questions' structure so that they are easier to ask.

-If your questions need changing or clarifying, rewrite the questions.

-Look at what you do with your hands. Do you naturally put them in your pockets while you talk? Don't, it looks too casual. Psychology says that people think you are hiding something when you put your hands in your pockets.

-Do you cross your arms? Don't, psychology says that this creates a barrier between you and the other person. To some people, they will read those actions negatively. They will think you are not interested, not receptive to their answers or just plain hostile.

-Practice keeping your arms relaxed by your side.

-What are you hands doing? Are you hands tightly clenched? Relax you hand and open you fingers. People read cues about you. A clenched hand could mean nervousness, or make you look like an uptight or angry person, and you don't want to give off that impression.

Dressing for the gallery meeting.

1. Casual dress is the norm these days so dress in good clothes that are clean and tidy.

2. Make sure that your shoes are clean.

3. No funky hats. You want to look professional but a casual version of professional.

Decide what you will wear and write it down here:

1._____

_____

_____

_____

2._____

_____

_____

_____

3. _____

_____

_____

_____

4. _____

_____

_____

_____

5. _____

_____

_____

_____

Participating in an art fair, art festival or art sale

There are many kinds of fairs or art festivals and again - its best to start close to home. You are more likely to know some of the artists participating. You may even know some of the organizers.

Make a list of the art fairs or art festivals near you. I encourage you to visit these art fairs or festivals before you apply.

List your top three here. Beside each one, list why you like this particular fair or festival:

1._____

_____

_____

_____

2._____

_____

_____

_____

3._____

_____

_____

_____

Applying for an art fair or festival

All art fairs or art festivals have application forms. Generally, the application form needs to be filled out and handed in about six months before the event. Most application forms are online. Regularly check into the festival's website to see any updates about the application period. Keep this in mind:

1. The forms usually take a long time to fill out. Allow one or two days for this process.

2. Have the material they want ready before you actually fill out the form. This information often needs to be loaded electronically.

3. Have good visual material ready. High quality digital images of your work are a must. Most forms ask for a JPG format.

4. Each image should have your name, title of the work, the medium, the size and the price. If you don't know how to do this, learn how.

5. Most images need to be formatted to a certain size. Learn to do this too.

6. The organizers will ask why you want to join this group, think about your answer. Craft it with as much care as you did your artist statement. The organizers have a particular goal in mind, so make sure your work is compatible with the art fair or art festival. For example, they might want to promote only local artists or only contemporary artists. Find out what their goal might be and write your information accordingly.

7. Try to meet some of the artists in the group you want to join. You can learn more about the group and you may be able to get a recommendation from one of them.

8. Read the application form carefully. Follow the instructions exactly or you will be eliminated immediately. Do not say 'this is good enough', it won't be. They will not look at your work if there are any part missing or badly done.

9. Be serious about how you present yourself.

The interview for the show

Some groups conduct interviews before bringing on new members. They will ask you about your work. Mostly, they want to see how you are in a public situation.

Read the section on *Approaching Galleries*. There, I give pointers on how to prepare for an interview. All the information in the that section also applies to this interview.

1. You need to create practice questions that they may ask.

2. Practice the relaxation techniques mentioned in the gallery section.

3. The interview may be via Skype. Find a spot in your house that is tidy and looks professional. Have a quiet spot where you will not be interrupted. If you have a dog, make sure he/she is not there and barking during the interview. Mute your telephone... I am sure you get the picture here, just be professional.

4. Make sure you have visited the art fair or festival to gain some basic knowledge as points of discussion in your interview.

5. Keep in mind that there is often a fee for participating in group fairs.

6. Each fair has a particular set-up style. You will need lights, a board or grid wall to hang your artwork on (pedestals for sculptural work). There are several requirements that are often not listed. Make sure you ask about these ahead

of time, talk to other artists to find out as much as you can, and budget for these items.

7. You will need to supply a list of the works you will show and their prices.

8. You will need to make labels for each work listing the title, medium and price. You need to create these ahead of time.

9. Having your logo on the labels is a good idea, it adds to your brand.

10. You may be asked to share your mailing list with the group because they will want to invite your clients. Or, they might ask you to do the promotion yourself. The group will outline exactly what they want you to do. Social media is usually involved, make sure you know how to promote yourself on at least one platform.

Make a list of the things you will do or learn to get ready here:

1._____

_____

_____

_____

2._____

_____

_____

_____

3._____

_____

_____

_____

4._____

_____

_____

5._____

_____

_____

_____

6._____

_____

_____

_____

Hosting your own show or open house

You can create your own art show by inviting people to your studio. Your studio can be in or out of your home.

There are many ways to approach an open studio. You can invite friends and family to come see and buy your work. You can add to this by handing out flyers to your neighbours and inviting them too.

Here are the steps I suggest that you follow:

1. Pick a date for your show/open house

2. Create your promotion material. This will include flyers and social media posts. Creating a Facebook event is a good idea.

3. You want to spread the word about a week to ten days ahead of time.

4. You will need to create a series of posts on social media for your show. For example, ten days before your show, you announce the open house by showing a visual of your work. Each day after this, make a short posts about things like your studio as you tidy it up, placing a painting on the wall, putting the finishing touches on a work, framing or simply posting a photo of your table full of paintings. Only show parts of the work and not the whole painting. These are called teasers.

5. The day before the show/open house, show an image/wide shot of your studio all ready to go. In bold type, announce that the show is TOMORROW.

6. You can create the photos in advance to make sure they ready to go. Just don't start posting them until 10 days before the event. This creates

a sense of urgency and puts you and your work in the minds of the people who see the posts.

7. Get rid of the clutter in your studio, make it look clean and tidy. You may have to hide things under the table, you can use a big tablecloth that goes to the floor to hide it all. This is what most artists do.

8. Read the section on *Approaching Galleries* about relaxation techniques and practice this.

9. Have a short 1 minute speech about your work. Practice this ahead of time in the mirror. Write up the core of your speech here:

_____

_____

_____

_____

_____

_____

_____

_____

_____

_____

_____

_____

_____

_____

_____

_____

_____

_____

_____

10. Practice smiling without looking nervous or stressed. Make it look casual and relaxed.

11. Put soft music on in the background and keep the volume low.

Sample Checklist

1. How many pieces of artwork do I have on the theme I want to market? Are they high quality?

Are they what I want to represent me? How many artworks do I need to make to meet my goal? Did you create a series of artworks that you want to promote? You need between 8 and 20 pieces for a series. Do you have that? It is a good idea to prepare the series before you start selling or applying for a show in a gallery.

2. If your are applying to have a solo show, how many works do you need to apply? Some galleries need 10 artworks and others may need as many as 40 artworks. Look at the gallery plan. You may be able to have 10 ready now and ask for a spot later in the year in order to get more work done by then. Keep in mind that you have a better chance at getting accepted if you have the work ready to go. You can say that the work is gallery ready and you can show any time. If they have an artist that cancels their show, you can be the artist that they choose.

3. Are the works ready to hang in a gallery? Make a list of what you need to do in order to 'finish off'

the work. For example, you may need to add wires on every painting or make sure you have an inventory of the work on your computer.

4. Do you have the work photographed and documented in a way that fulfills most shows' submissions requirements?

5. Do you have the application form downloaded, read and filled in?

6. Do your have the introduction letter written?

7. Do you have the lights and the grid wall to hang your work at the art fair? If you don't, do you have the money to buy those items? How can you save in order to get them?

8. You may need business cards or handouts. Do you have them ready? Do you need to make them or have someone do them for you? Have you figured out how much that will cost and can you afford them yet?

9. Do you have transportation for all your artwork or items you need for the show or the fair? If not, can you borrow one or rent some? Do you have money set aside for this?

10. If you are hanging artwork in your home or studio, do you have a way to hang the work? Are you allowed to put holes in the walls? If not, how will you hang the work?

11. Do you have a price list of your work? You should have this for any event.

12. Do you have labels for your artwork? Are they printed and ready to go?

13. Do you have a 'float' with change ready when you sell an artwork for cash? Do you a machine to take credit cards? Keep in mind that you have to pay a fee to the credit card company and you may have to adjust your prices to make sure you are making enough money. Check out how much the company charges.

14. Have you picked out the clothing you will wear for the event? Get the clothing ready so that you don't have to find something at the last minute. Make sure your clothing is comfortable as well as professional.

The list can be long but slowly check off every item. Being prepared will reduce your stress levels and you will smile in a happy, stress free way. You will not have to smile through thoughts like 'I wish that I had done this....or that....'.

What if only a few people visit?

This is a possibility; it happens to everyone. Be nice to those people who come, they will spread the word about your work and next time, more people will come. Word of mouth is the best way to promote the quality of your artwork.

A smile will win more hearts than anything else.

Your first clients will be your loyal ones.

Keep an upbeat attitude, praise the people that came. Really promote those people. Tell a story about how you talked to them for hours and now they really understand your work.

To consider:

Ask the people who do come to your show or open house to write a short comment that you can post on social media. Ask permission to put their name on it. If they don't, put the: "Today, one of my clients said.."

These testimonials are important because they are comments about your professional abilities. Add them to your website and your blogs. Note: Even if they are your cousin, that is OK, no one will know you are related!

Make a list of the things you will do to get ready here:

1._____

_____

_____

_____

2._____

_____

_____

_____

3._____

_____

_____

_____

4._____

_____

_____

_____

5._____

_____

_____

_____

6._____

_____

_____

7._____

_____

_____

_____

8._____

_____

_____

_____

9._____

_____

_____

_____

10._____

_____

_____

_____

_____

If your list is longer, just add a piece of paper to this page.

More ideas here:

CHAPTER 9

ANALYZE THE COMPETITION

It is essential to know who the other artists creating work similar to yours are. This allows you to keep up with what is selling and what is not. You also need to know what prices they are selling at and where they are selling. Your competition will be doing the same thing, they will be researching you!

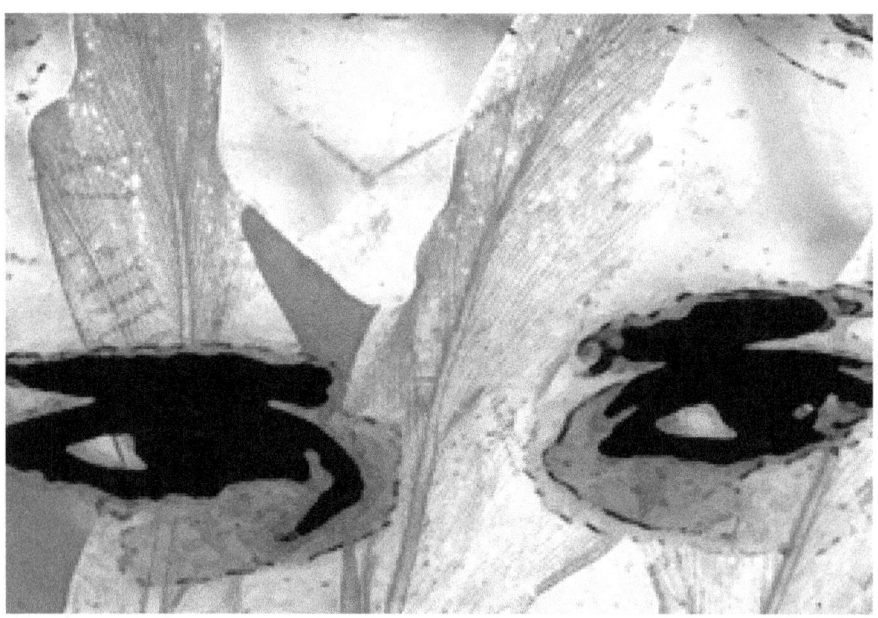

The look   By Doris Charest

As you move from a beginner to professional artist, selling becomes more important. You are now competing against others for buyers. There are are a finite amount of sales that artists are competing for. Knowing who your competitors are and what they are offering can help you make your artwork, services and marketing stand out. It will enable you to set your prices competitively and help you to respond to rival marketing campaigns with your own initiatives.

Think of building your knowledge of other artists' work as research.

1. You are researching what works and what does not.

2. You will find out if the type of artwork you are creating is a growing market (trends do happen

in the art world) or is tapped out because too many people have decided to paint that topic.

3. You find out if your paintings are at the right price point or priced too high or low.

This research is similar to the research you did to find the right gallery or art fair. You need to identify which artists are your competitors, find out what they are doing and how they are selling.

You can use this information to:

-help you find new venues for you

-price your work competitively

-better direct your energies towards activities that will lead to sales

-guide you to better sales practices

-guide you to new galleries

-lead you to better marketing ideas.

You can think of your competitors as mentors, they can guide you to better practices and a better art business.

To start this process you need to;

1. Find artists that work in your style.

2. Find artists who work your subject matter.

Write down the names of these artists here. Next to the name write what they do.

_____

_____

_____

_____

_____

_____

_____

_____

_____

_____

_____

_____

_____

_____

_____

Now you need to find out where and how they sell.
List the ways here :

_____

_____

_____

_____

_____

_____

_____

_____

_____

_____

_____

Where do these artists list their work on the
internet? List the venues here. For example, they
show with the Federation of Canadian Artists,
Saachi, Society 6, Etsy or Deviant Art.

_____

_____

_____

_____

_____

_____

_____

_____

_____

_____

Which of these venues are the most popular? Do
some research to find out if they are for show or

for sales. Write those down here with an indication
if they are for show or sales:

_____

_____

_____

_____

_____

_____

_____

_____

_____

_____

_____

_____

_____

_____

_____

_____

_____

CHAPTER 10

SET GOALS

Goals give you guidelines, they help you get organized and move forwards. You can set up weekly, monthly, yearly or five (or more) year goals.

Brush photo by D. Charest

While your business might always be changing, if you set at least basic goals they will help you grow your business with purpose. not. You also need to know what prices they are selling at and where they are selling. Your competition will be doing the same thing, they will be researching you!

Start with long range goals.

Most artists rarely go beyond a 5 year plan. The art business is always changing and this means that your goals will change, but you can still make 20 year goals. You will just need to revisit them regularly.

The longer the goal, the more high level it should be. For example, a twenty year goal would be to sell your florals to across the country or to sell

artwork internationally or to participate in a
European biennale. These are broad goals.

Write your long term goals here:

1._____

_____

_____

_____

_____

_____

_____

_____

_____

_____

_____

2._____

_____

_____

_____

_____

_____

3.

_____

_____

4. _____

_____

_____

_____

_____

_____

_____

_____

_____

_____

5. _____

_____

_____

_____

_____

_____

_____

_____

_____

Identify *one goal* to keep from these exercises. Having one long term goal will help you have a focus and keep your eye on a 'prize'.

Write that goal here:

1._____

_____

_____

_____

One year goals

You have now picked your long term goal and you need to decide where you want to be in relation to that goal in one year.

For example, if I decide that I want to sell my florals across the country, how do I break that down in order to achieve some that goal this year? How can I start selling my florals now? What do I need to do to make that happen?

Here is a sample goal:

I want to exhibit in two group shows and have one solo show in one calendar year. To achieve this goal, I need to:

Create a body of work on one theme that I want to show.

Find galleries that may be interested in my work. This can be done after you have visited the galleries to see what kind of work they usually accept.

Download the application forms, read them and fill out the paperwork.

Photograph all my current series and have the JPGs ready and labeled

Send in the application before the date deadline.

Wait for their reply and have work ready to show.

Note: You can show the same work in each art show. What you need to make sure is that you have enough work to fill the spaces you are applying to. If your series has twelve 16 x 20 in. pieces, for example, a gallery with 700 linear feet of wall, is going to be too big. But if you have thirty 24 x 24 in. pieces, you probably have have enough work.

CHAPTER 11

VISIBILITY AND SELF PROMOTION

In this section you will decide on at least two ways you can start to promote yourself. The first steps are getting to know new people, getting to know gallery owners and getting to know clients. This is called networking. Networking is a great way to get known as an artist.

Art supply photo by D. Charest

Getting known...

Getting known is often seen as a big mystery. However, there are small steps you can take that will get you started in the right direction. These are different ways to gain notoriety. I will run you through a list of possibilities, not all of them may be applicable to you. Your local art scene may not have groups for you to join. There may not be local shows for you to join. You may not like teaching but love working the internet or vice versa. Read through the possibilities and add your own to the list.

Option #1

First and foremost, visit other artists, galleries and art activities for the love of it; not for pitching your work, get to know people first. Get them to know you, and make friends. Save your pitch for later.

Show interest by collecting business cards from the people you meet. Find out about other artists in your area. Send an email or a card as a follow-up, and be sure to mention the meeting. Set up a future meeting with your best connections; artists or business people.

Visit all the galleries in your area, and get to know the owners. Attend as many openings as possible. This is not to promote your own work (there will be time enough for that later) but to become a known artist in the community.

Option #2

Join fine art societies and enter contests. Start off with student level or small local art contests.

If there are no art groups in your area, create one. Ask the artists you know to help. If there are no art clubs and art societies to join in your area and you want support from other artists, this is a great opportunity. You can start by creating a painting group, for example, where you paint together every Monday. As the group grows, you form a formal society with an executive.

Option #3

Teach workshops. This will help you not only get known as an artist, but also as an expert in your field.

Option #4

Enter juried art shows. Getting a painting into a juried art show is itself an achievement to put on your resume. When you have too many, shorten it by listing only the most important shows. Remember what I said earlier, keep a master document of ALL your shows and then select the ones you want to put on your short resume.

Option #5

Art Agents are people who represent you and sell your work to large companies or licensing companies and even galleries. Many people advise that beginners need an art agent. Bad news here, agents are not applicable for beginners. Very few reps want to work with beginners. They want someone with a good reputation already. Read up on art agencies and agents but do not make finding an agent one of your first priorities. He/she will ask what you have done to promote yourself and how you can help them promote yourself. Once you are a mid-career artist you may consider an art agent, but you should already know how to promote yourself better.

Option #6

Make a pop-up show. Ask a local business if you can set up a table in their business. Ask others to join you and set up for the day. Make sure that you have a way to collect emails so you contact each other to work together again.

A few more ideas

Apply for a booth at the local trade show, you can do this because you are a business.

Hold a show in your own home. I discuss this in a different chapter.

Hold a garden art show. Set up artwork in your garden then invite everyone to come see both the garden and the artwork.

These are just ideas. Write you own ideas here:

_____

_____

_____

_____

_____

_____

_____

_____

_____

_____

_____

_____

_____

_____

_____

_____

Different ways to get known

1. *When you have a show or participate in a group show, contact the local reporter and tell them about it. Include a photo of your work with the announcement.*

2. *Apply to put your work in shop windows with their own products. I had one shop owner let me show my work on the walls of her boutique.*

3. *Local libraries sometimes have spots to show artwork. Ask your local librarian.*

CHAPTER 12

TO BLOG OR NOT TO BLOG

In this section, you will make decisions about blogging. Blogging on art can be fun. Here are some tips on getting started.

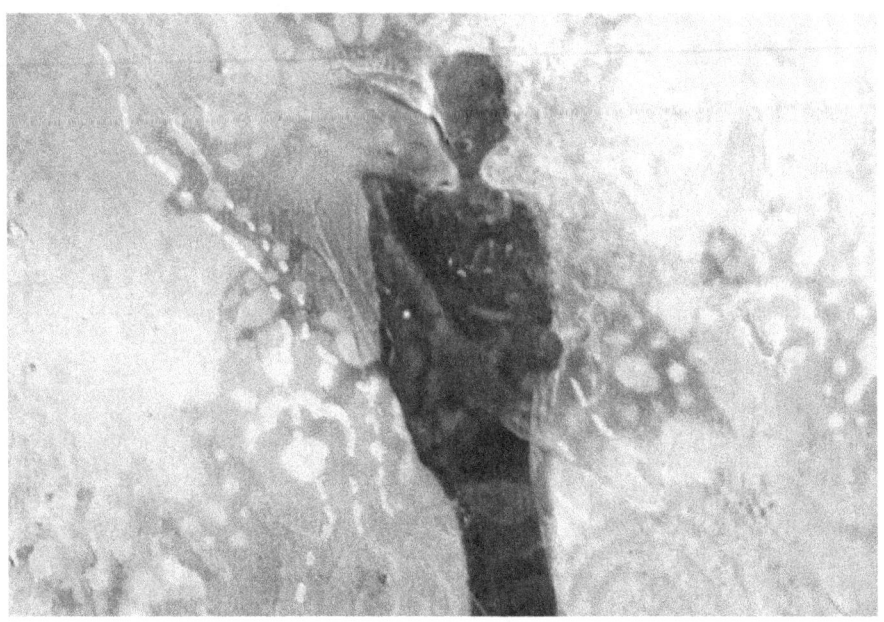

Alone out there   by D. Charest

Blogging involves writing articles about your work and can be a good way of getting your name known. Many artists struggle with writing, so keep in mind that you do not have to create a blog, it is only one of many ways to be discovered by new people.

If you like writing, just start. Posting regularly is important to gather a following. Quality regular posts are good but irregular good posts are not. Even once a month is better than irregular posts. A blog is a discussion or informational website published on the internet consisting of discrete, often informal diary-style text entries that are called posts.

The posts can be about anything but usually touch a topic important to the author. If you want to blog about art, you should write posts related to your work and medium you love.

Here are some of the most popular platforms available:

1. WordPress.org

2. Wix .com

3. WordPress.com

4. Blogger.com

5. Tumblr.com

6. Medium.com

7. Squarespace.com

8. Joomla.com

Blogging can be seen as a form of social networking. Bloggers do not only produce content to post on their websites, but also often build connections with their readers and other bloggers.

Many blogs provide commentary on a particular subject or topic, ranging from politics to sports.

Others blogs types include personal online diaries or online brand advertising of a particular individual or company. A typical blog combines text, digital images, and links to other blogs, web pages, and other media related to its topic.

Most blogs are primarily text, although some focus on art (art blogs), photographs (photoblogs), videos (video blogs or "vlogs"), music (MP3 blogs), and audio (podcasts).

In education, blogs can be used as instructional resources. These blogs are referred to as edu-blogs. Microblogging is another type of blogging, featuring very short posts.

Blogs can be short story collections, recipe hubs, role-playing games, or records of UFO sightings. They can help businesses advertise, educate customers, inform shareholders, or inspire community interactions.

Today, we have all kinds of platforms for blogs. Linking your blog to your website is essential. Some websites offer blogging platforms so this may be an item that you want to add to what you want on your website.

Decide what you would like your blog to be about. Do you want to talk about your daily art journey or do you want to educate others about art? Write down your goals for your blog here:

_____

_____

_____

_____

_____

_____

_____

Once you have your idea, you need topics you can write about. If, for example, you decide that you want to educate others about art and pencil work in particular, you might blog about:

-Where to find good art materials

-How to find an art supply store in your area

-The difference between a HB pencil and a 2B pencil

-How to choose the right pencil for a certain drawing technique

-How to choose the right paper to draw on

-How to fix a drawing so it doesn't smear

What is the topic that you would like to blog on? Write it down here:

_____

_____

_____

_____

_____

_____

_____

_____

_____

_____

_____

_____

_____

_____

List at least ten elements of this topic that you can blog about:

1._____

_____

_____

2._____

_____

_____

_____

_____

3._____

_____

_____

_____

_____

4._____

_____

_____

_____

_____

5._____

_____

_____

_____

_____

6._____

_____

_____

_____

_____

7._____

_____

_____

_____

_____

8._____

_____

_____

_____

_____

9._____

_____

_____

10._____

_____

_____

_____

_____

Batch writing

Blogging can be fun. However, some people find it stressful. Planning ahead can help you stay consistent. Batch writing is when you sit down and write all ten of your blogs at once. Make your list and then start writing. Once all the blogs are done, you can space out the posts so they are released on a regular schedule.

I love this option because I only have to sit down to write every three months or so.

The first draft

Write without stopping. Don't correct your spelling or any of your words. Just write, let the words flow.

When you are done, use spellcheck and correct the errors. Leave it after this.

The second draft.

Two days later and no sooner, look at your writing and correct any grammar errors that you can now see.

This is the time to make any changes to the structure or content.

The third draft.

Double check your text another time.

At the end of the your writing session, make sure to ask someone to proof-read your work.

Scheduling

You can schedule your posts so that they come out without you having to think about it. You can have several months of posts scheduled and they will come out on their own. Often I schedule for up to three or four months at a time.

Blogging ideas

1. *Write about your favourite techniques*

2. *Write about your successes in your practice*

3. *Write about your art problems*

4. *Write about what it is like to participate in an art show*

5. *Write about joining an art group*

6. *Write about your art friends (with their permission)*

7. *Write about new things you try in your artwork*

8. *Write about your favourite artists*

CHAPTER 13

SOCIAL MEDIA BASICS

Social media is a big part of marketing. You DO need to start using it for your art business, but you SHOULD NOT use your personal account. You should have separate business accounts for all the social media sites. You can try different social media sites and choose the ones best for you. Let's look at a few options.

Art photo by D. Charest

Facebook

Facebook features:

- News Feed.

- Friends.

- Wall.

- Timeline.

- Likes and Reactions.

- Comments.

- Messages and inbox.

- Notifications.

- Photographs

- Videos

- Marketplace

- Events

- Live streaming

- Events

Facebook is essential for any business, and the platform makes it easy to create a business page.

Facebook is a multi-purpose social networking website where users can post comments, share photographs and post links to news or other interesting content on the web, chat live, and watch short-form video. You can even order food on Facebook! Shared content can be made publicly accessible, or it can be shared only among a select group of friends or family.

Facebook is user-friendly and open to everyone. Even the least technical-minded people can sign up and start posting on Facebook. Although it started out as a way to keep in touch or reconnect with long-lost friends, it rapidly became businesses' best way to be able to closely target audiences and deliver ads directly to the people most likely to want their products or services.

Facebook makes it simple to share photos, text messages, videos, status posts and feelings on. The site is entertaining and a regular daily stop for many users.

A major benefit of Facebook advertising is its ability to reach your exact audience. Facebook is the most targeted form of advertising. You can advertise to people by age, interests, behaviour, and location. If you really know your customers, you can use Facebook advertising to engage them.

Facebook provides a customizable set of privacy controls, so users can protect their information from getting to third-party individuals.

Key Features of Facebook

Facebook allows you to maintain an audience (your followers) list and choose privacy settings to tailor who can see content on your profile.

Facebook allows you to upload photos and maintain photo albums that can be shared with your clients and followers.

Facebook supports interactive onlinc chat and the ability to comment on your followers' profile pages to keep in touch, share information or to say "Hi."

Facebook supports group pages, fan pages, and business pages that let businesses use Facebook as a vehicle for social media marketing.

Facebook's developer network delivers advanced functionality and monetization options.

You can stream video live using Facebook Live.

Chat with Facebook friends and family members, or auto-display Facebook pictures with the Facebook Portal device.

Here is how you get started

Step 1: Get a Facebook business account.

Step 2: Get a good photo of yourself to put on the site.

Step 3: Pick an interesting painting that you can use as a background to your personal photo. Upload both.

Step 4: Post interesting content regularly. It doesn't have to be everyday, just make sure it is regular. If you can only post once a week and only on Friday, that is good enough. Recommendations from 'Social Media Gurus' say posting every single day is important. However, when you are a solo-preneur (creator of work, administrator and promoter all in one), this is not always realistic. Go for regular; a single time once a week and on the same day.

Step 5: Share other people's content on your page. This not only helps others but saves you from doing a ton of research for new material. For example, I repost good ideas from different galleries or museums.

List your ideas that you could post on Facebook here. Remember to keep in mind your overall goal with this page. You want to get people to know your work and promote art at the same time.

1._____

_____

_____

_____

_____

_____

2._____

_____

_____

3._____

_____

_____

_____

_____

_____

4._____

_____

_____

_____

_____

_____

5._____

_____

_____

_____

_____

_____

_____

If you are a printmaker, share content on
printmaking. If you are a sculptor, share sculpting

ideas and tips. Every once in a while, share something interesting from a painter or a fabric artist, for example, to help educate your public about art as a whole.

Find interesting artists on Facebook and 'like' them so that you can share some of their content. Do research and find at least three artists to follow. Write their names here, add why you like them.

1._____

_____

_____

_____

_____

2._____

_____

_____

_____

3._____

_____

_____

_____

_____

_____

Find three museums or art galleries that you would like to follow. Add their names here. Make sure to list why you like each of these choices.

1._____

_____

_____

_____

_____

_____

2._____

_____

_____

_____

_____

_____

_____

3._____

_____

_____

_____

_____

_____

4. _____

_____

_____

_____

_____

5. _____

_____

_____

_____

_____

_____

_____

_____

_____

Find three online art groups to follow. Write their names here. Make sure to list why you like each of these choices.

1._____

_____

_____

_____

2._____

_____

_____

_____

_____

_____

3._____

_____

_____

_____

_____

_____

4._____

_____

_____

_____

_____

_____

5._____

_____

_____

_____

_____

_____

_____

_____

_____

_____

Between the three artists, three galleries or museums and three art groups, you should be able to find content to share.

Instagram

Instagram is a photo-sharing app. There are many photo sharing platforms but Instagram is the best and has the most users. Instagram is known for its square image format, its lack of a website features and, of course, those nostalgic filters.

Similar to Facebook or Twitter, everyone who creates an Instagram account has a profile and a news feed.

Before you can start using the app, Instagram will ask you to create a free account. You can sign up via your existing Facebook account or by email. All you need is a username and a password.

You may be asked if you want to follow some friends who are on Instagram in your Facebook network. You can do this right away or skip through the process and come back to it later.

It's always a good idea to customize your profile by adding your name, a photo, a short bio and a website link if you have one when you first get on Instagram. When you start following people and looking for people to follow you back, they'll want to know who you are and what you're all about.

When you post a photo or video on Instagram, it will be displayed on your profile. Other users who follow you will see your posts in their own feed. Likewise, you'll see posts from other users whom you choose to follow.

Instagram is like a simplified version of Facebook, with an emphasis on mobile use and visual sharing. Just like other social networks, you can interact with other users on Instagram by following them, being followed by them, commenting, liking, tagging and private messaging. You can even save the photos you see on Instagram.

Devices That Work With Instagram

Instagram is available for free on iOS devices, like the iPhone and iPad, as well as Android devices, like phones and tablets from Google, Samsung, etc.

It can also be accessed on the web from a computer, but users can only upload and share photos or videos from their phones.

As previously mentioned, Instagram is all about visual sharing, so everybody's main intention is to share and find only the best photos and videos. Every user profile has "Followers", which represents how many people are following them, then "Following", how many they are following.

Every user profile has a button you can tap to follow them. If a user has their profile set to private, they will need to approve your request first.

Keep in mind that when your profile is created and set to public, anyone can find and view your profile, along with all your photos and videos. Learn how to set yours to private if you only want the followers you approve to be able to see your posts.

Interacting on posts is fun and easy. You can double tap any post to "like" it or add a comment at the bottom. You can even click the arrow button to share it with someone via direct message.

You can create post both directly through the app or from existing photos/videos on your device. You can also post both photos and videos up to one full minute in length, and there are plenty of extra filter options plus the ability to tweak and edit.

Sharing Your Instagram Posts

Once you have a photo and made the necessary edits, then you are now ready to post. You'll be taken to a tab where you can fill out a caption, tag other users to it, tag it to a geographical location and simultaneously post it to some of your other social networks.

You can configure your Instagram account to have photos posted on Facebook, Twitter, Tumblr or Flickr.

Instagram also has a Stories feature, which is a secondary feed that appears at the very top of your main feed. You can see it marked by little photo bubbles of the users you follow.

Tap any one of these bubbles to see that user's story or stories that they published over the last 24 hours, they disappear at the end of the 24 hours. To publish your own story, all you have to do is tap your own photo bubble from the main feed or swipe right on any tab to access the stories camera tab.

Your goal is to follow the same steps as you did with Facebook. Pick three artists, three galleries or museums and three groups to join. They don't have to be the same as the Facebook ones.

List the kind of content that interests you.

_____

_____

_____

_____

_____

_____

_____

_____

_____

_____

_____

Why does it interest you?

_____

_____

_____

_____

_____

_____

_____

_____

_____

_____

_____

_____

_____

_____

_____

_____

_____

_____

Do some research and find at least three artists to follow. Write their names here. Add why you like them.

1._____

_____

_____

_____

_____

2._____

_____

_____

_____

_____

3._____

_____

_____

_____

_____

Find three museums or art galleries that you would like to follow. Add their names here. Make sure to list why you like each of these choices.

1._____

_____

_____

_____

_____

_____

2._____

_____

_____

_____

_____

_____

3._____

_____

_____

_____

_____

_____

4._____

_____

_____

_____

_____

_____

5._____

_____

_____

_____

_____

_____

_____

_____

Find three online art groups to follow. Write their names here. Make sure to list why you like each of these choices.

1._____

_____

_____

_____

_____

_____

2._____

_____

_____

_____

_____

_____

3._____

_____

_____

_____

_____

_____

4._____

_____

_____

_____

_____

5._____

_____

_____

_____

_____

Between the three artists, three galleries or
museums and three art groups, you should be able
to find content to share.

Twitter

Twitter is used to connect people with the same interests through text.

You can get up to the minute updates on the things that interest you like politics, the economy, entertainment and art.

The short nature of tweets means that Twitter is widely used by smartphone users who don't want to read long content items on-screen. Twitter allows you to: easily promote your information links to your blog stories, journal articles and news items like your current show that starts tomorrow.

Twitter's big appeal is how easy to read it is. You can track hundreds of interesting Twitter users and read their content quickly in a few lines of text.

Twitter employs a message size restriction to keep things short: every tweet entry is limited to 280 characters or less. This size restriction made Twitter a popular tool.

How Twitter Works

Twitter is easy to use. You join with a free account and Twitter name. Then you send tweets daily, hourly, or as frequently as you like. Go to the What's Happening box, type 280 or fewer characters, and click Tweet. People who follow you, and potentially others who don't, will see your tweet.

Encourage people you know to follow you and receive your tweets in their Twitter feeds. Let your friends know you are on Twitter to slowly build up a following. When people follow you, Twitter etiquette calls for you to follow them back.

To receive Twitter feeds, find someone interesting (celebrities included) and press Follow to subscribe to their tweets. You can unfollow if the tweets end up not being entertaining. You can go to your account at Twitter.com day or night to read your Twitter feed, which is constantly updating.

Twitter as a Marketing Tool

Thousands of people advertise their recruiting services, consulting businesses, and retail stores by using Twitter, and it works. People prefer advertising that is fast, less intrusive, and can be turned on or off at will.

Twitter as a Social Messaging Tool

Twitter is about discovering interesting people around the world. It can also be about building a following of people who are interested in you and your work or hobbies and then providing those followers with some knowledge value every day.

Twitter Is Many Different Things

Twitter is a blend of instant messaging, blogging, and texting, but with brief content and a broad audience. If you fancy yourself a bit of a writer with something to say, then Twitter is one way to connect with those people or topic.

Let's practice.

I will give you a description and you will tweet something short and to the point.

You want to talk about your up and coming show in two days time. The show will be at the XYZ Gallery on Lamont Street in Ottawa. This is a big moment for you, you are very excited. You theme is horses and you titled the work 'Mane Attraction'. The work is semi-abstract in bold colours and is done in acrylic. Write a tweet with 280 characters or less.

_____

_____

_____

_____

_____

_____

Here is a second exercise for you. You have just finished a series of photographs of back alleys in Nice, France. This was done on a trip two years ago. Your focus is the beautiful doors. Not only are the doors in a variety of colours but there are elaborate designs on most of the doors. Your title is 'Not Quite Shut'. You are not sure you chose the right title but it is the title now. The series is your best work so far. You have 280 characters to tweet the essence of this information.

_____

_____

_____

_____

Describe your next show. Include lots of
information.

_____

_____

_____

_____

_____

_____

_____

_____

_____

_____

_____

_____

_____

_____

_____

Write a short tweet about **this** show here in 280
characters or less:

_____

_____

_____

_____

_____

_____

_____

_____

What image would you use with this tweet?

_____

_____

_____

Short and sweet is the key to Twitter tweets. Make sure you use very short clear, concise words that describe precisely what you want to say.

Review: Twitter is great for:

Short messages

Announcing an art show

Announcing an art event

Announcing the publication of your art book

Announcing an opening

Announcing your classes

Announcing your new videos

Announcing an art related activity that you want people to come to. Send it the day before and the day of the activity.

Youtube

Youtube is a website for sharing videos. Many artists use Youtube for promoting their art shows and teaching art lessons.

To help connect users to the videos they are looking for, YouTube uses a complex algorithm made up of over one million lines of code.

When you search for a video, the algorithm decides which search results it will show you and in what order. One of the main factors used to rank the results is video metadata.

Millions of users around the world have created accounts on the site that allow them to upload videos that anyone can watch. Every minute of every day, more than 35 hours of video is uploaded to YouTube.

Video files can be very large and are often too big to send to someone else by email. By posting a video on YouTube, you can share a video simply by sending the other person a url 'link' – that is, the 'address' of the relevant internet page.

When YouTube was created in 2005, it was intended for people to post and share original video content. But since then it's also become both an archive for storing favourite clips, songs and jokes, as well as a marketing site for companies to promote their products.

Artists and YouTube

Most artists use Youtube to share small promotional videos when they have art shows or events, this means learning how to make videos. Keep your promotional videos around a minute, most people's attention spans are short so half hour promotional videos won't work.

Keep your style and brand in mind when you are creating these videos. If you are a pencil artist, for example, you can create a video explaining the difference between HB pencils and 6B pencils then send them to your website to see your work.

List some ideas for promotional videos here. Write next to them, why these videos would promote your work.

1._____

_____

_____

_____

_____

2._____

_____

_____

_____

_____

_____

3._____

_____

_____

_____

4._____

_____

_____

_____

_____

_____

5._____

_____

_____

_____

Which of these ideas appeal to you the most at this moment? Write it down here. List the steps you need to take in order to make this video. You may need to borrow your friends' iPhone, if you don't have one. You may need to move a table and set up in a well lit area with a lot of daylight. Write your steps here:

1._____

_____

_____

_____

2._____

_____

_____

3._____

_____

_____

4._____

_____

_____

5._____

_____

_____

Getting started is the hardest part. Start now.

10 Things You Need to Do When Getting Started on YouTube

1. Think about what you want to achieve. Before you do anything, you need to figure out what you're hoping to get out of building a presence on YouTube.

2. Create your channel.

3. Create playlists.

4. Share your content.

5. Analyze your data.

6. Stay engaged with your audience.

7. Link to your Google+ Account.

8. Create an account to share videos up to 15 minutes long with your family and friends. You can upload videos that are longer than

15 minutes if you follow steps to verify your account. There is a guide to doing this on the YouTube Help pages.

9. Use the YouTube edit facility to create a movie with music and other features.

10. Restrict who views your videos with YouTube's privacy option.

Nowadays the term 'viral video' is common. This refers to a video clip that people have liked so much that they've shared it with millions of others around the globe.

Companies have realized that they can harness this ability to reach potential customers and have created their own YouTube accounts for posting advertisements and other marketing videos.

YouTube is great for:

Showing videos of your artwork

Showing a video of your latest show

Showing a video of your latest art event

Showing a sample of the class you are hosting either live or online.

Showing a video of you in your studio at work on any kind of artwork. People love seeing artists at work.

Showing a video of you painting live (taken by someone else)

Showing a video of just your studio as messy as it may be. People love this.

Snapchat

Snapchat is an image and video messaging app.

One of the principal features of Snapchat is that pictures and messages are usually only available for a short time before they become inaccessible to their recipients. The app has evolved from originally focusing on person-to-person photo sharing to presently featuring users' "Stories" of 24 hours of chronological content, along with "Discover", letting brands show ad-supported short-form content.

Snapchat intended for one-on-one conversations. Your friend is giving you their full attention. Snapchat added stickers, easier access to audio and video conferencing, the ability to leave audio or video "notes", and the ability to share recent camera photos.

I have to admit that I did not choose Snapchat as part of my social media choices for marketing my art. However, this does not mean that you shouldn't. If you already have a strong following on Snapchat, use it for your art marketing.

Follow the same steps as with Facebook and Instagram if you choose this site.

List the kind of content that interests you. You can find the content using hashtags.

List the kind of content that interests you.

_____

_____

_____

_____

_____

_____

_____

_____

_____

Why does it interest you?

_____

_____

_____

_____

_____

_____

_____

_____

_____

_____

Do some research and find at least three artists to follow. Write their names here. Add why you like them.

1._____

_____

_____

_____

_____

2._____

_____

_____

_____

_____

3._____

_____

_____

_____

_____

_____

_____

Find three museums or art galleries that you would like to follow. Add their names here. Make sure to list why you like each of these choices.

1._____

_____

_____

_____

_____

2._____
_____
_____
_____
_____
_____

3._____
_____
_____
_____
_____
_____
_____
_____

4._____
_____
_____
_____
_____

5._____
_____
_____

_____

_____

_____

_____

_____

_____

_____

Find three online art groups to follow. Write their names here. Make sure to list why you like each of these choices.

1._____

_____

_____

_____

_____

2._____

_____

_____

_____

_____

3._____

_____

_____

_____

_____

_____

4._____

_____

_____

_____

_____

5._____

_____

_____

_____

_____

_____

_____

Between the three artists, three galleries or museums and three art groups, you should be able to find content to share.

This is an app with a difference.

With this app, once you have seen the message, it disappears.

If you are sending a photo, it is the same.

If you create an add that you put on this app, you will have to resend it regularly.

The concept is to send new and exciting ideas or messages.

Other ways to sell your art online

Selling online is another way to get your name known. There are several third party sites where you can list your work. You can put your image on a cup or a t-shirt or sell copies of your work.

Selling this way, by not creating new pieces but using old ones in multiple ways, is sometimes called 'passive income'.

Sounds easy, doesn't it? But, like any other product, you still have to do some marketing. The sites will promote their site but it is up to the artist to promote their own products.

You need to decide if you have time to do this type of promotion. This is work that you have to do on top of creating your work.

Reproductions or copies:

Where you choose to sell your work will depend on your style and the kind of work you do. You can start selling online with companies that are already established. This allows you to take advantage of an existing audiences as well as an existing sales tools, without the need of develop neither by yourself.

You have to decide what you want:

Do you want to sell only originals?

Do you want to sell copies of your work?

Do you want to sell copies of your work on t-shirts or cups?

If you are an illustrator or have bright coloured work that is more design oriented then maybe creating a merchandising line is a good move. Some companies offer print on demand, other are online art galleries or art commission websites. Make a list of each of their main points so that later you can decide which you prefer.

Before starting with any of these platforms you should do your research and analyze which ones best fit your art practice. Take the time to look at them all. Some have higher price points, some pay for shipping while some charge a lot for shipping.

I suggest starting on one platform and getting used to it. Tell all you friends and clients about it. Use it for a while and see if it performs well for you. If it doesn't, drop it and try another.

If you decide to be a part on several platforms at the same time it's important to make sure there are some similarities between the two:

1.You pricing should be the same on every platform, if someone buys an artwork and then sees it for a cheaper price on another website, they will feel cheated. They will not buy from you again.

1. Have an inventory sheet so you can have a complete overview of what artworks are being listed on each site so you don't risk selling the same artwork twice.

Write down what kinds of sale possibilities that you are interested in here:

1._____

_____

_____

_____

_____

_____

2._____

_____

_____

_____

_____

_____

_____

3._____

_____

_____

_____

_____

_____

4._____

_____

_____

_____

_____

_____

Here are some sites for you to explore. Keep in mind that sites change frequently and that your job is to stay up to date. As I write this, these are the popular sites:

ArtPal is a popular, free gallery to buy art and to sell art, representing many thousands of artists. You can sell originals, prints or use their free print-on-demand service. It's also quick and easy to set up.

Artfinder is a juried gallery, with a great selection of artists. They regularly feature artists from their network (this part is very good), giving them extra visibility. They also have a ranking of artists, updated weekly. Research what you need to do to be ranked, sometimes you need to pay.

Saatchii is one of the biggest art marketplaces out there. They organize art fairs, curator groups and actively promote artists. The site offers more than 500,000 original paintings, drawings, sculptures and photographs by over 50,000 emerging artists from over 100 countries. It is the largest gallery and platform for artists in the world.

Society6 is an online marketplace that lets artists sell their artwork on a variety of products. It is an online print-on-demand website that allows you to upload your artwork and turn it into a large number of products. Using the platform you will be able to transform your artworks into phone cases, stickers, t-shirts, shower curtains and of course posters & prints. This way you can sell to a broader audience.

Society6 automatically generates product images without you having to adjust your design size and preparc mockups for cvcry product you want to sell. The only thing you need to worry about figuring out is how to direct your followers to your store on Society6, or how to get found in Society6 search.

If you want to have more control over the products you sell and price tag you put on them, you should consider opening an online store with **Printful**, an online drop shipping and custom print fulfillment service. With Society6, prices are pre-determined by the site and you make 10% of each sale (with the exception of art prints, which the artist prices).

Artquid is an online art gallery for artists to upload and sell their art. The main difference is that Artquid allows artists to create a 3D gallery that allows collectors to really visualize the artworks.

DeviantArt is an online artwork, videography and photography community. Artworks are organized in a category structure, including photography, digital art, traditional art, literature, flash, filmmaking, skins for applications, operating system customization utilities and others, along with downloadable resources such as tutorials and stock photography. Additional features include "journals", "polls", "groups" and "portfolios". This is a big online site.

Members of DeviantArt may leave comments and critiques on individual pages and have the option to share through social media (Facebook, Twitter, etc.).

Individual members can organize their own folders on their personal pages.

Amazon is a place to buy and sell pretty much anything, and it's one of the largest e-commerce platforms out there.

eBay - on eBay merchants compete over various product offerings like electronics and sporting goods. eBay has a popular collectibles and art section where you can find antiques, art, coins, comics, sport memorabilia and other collectibles.

Etsy is one of the greatest creative marketplaces online for buying and selling art and other unique goods. On Etsy you can set up your own store to sell your designs, paintings, sculptures, photography, prints and additional artwork. Also, if you're lucky, your art or shop could be featured in the Etsy blog leading to new exposure and likely sales.

Zazzle is a marketplace for buying and selling custom art, clothes, electronics and other products. The Zazzle "Make Engine" is a tool and marketplace for customizing just about anything you can imagine from posters to t-shirts to coffee mugs. You can keep up with interesting designs and artist's on the Zazzle blog.

CafePress is a place to buy and sell mugs and other drink ware along with t-shirts, stationary and wall art. I also like to keep up with CafeStyle, the CafePress blog about designers, trends, product spotlights and deals.

Redbubble is a place to buy and sell t-shirts, towels, scarves, and other items like wall art. This is a great place to test putting your artwork on items useful in the home and on clothing. With Redbubble, you decide your own price above the base price and you pocket the difference.

Fine Art America - if you're looking for museum quality prints, canvases, frames, acrylics, metal prints and other poster materials, check out Fine Art America. The site helps you create a business around your art and photography by printing and assembling your orders while handling all the packaging, shipping and everything needed to get your art to the customer.

List 5 possible sites that you can use to promote your work.

1. _____
_____
_____

2. _____
_____
_____

3. _____
_____
_____

4. _____

_____

_____

5. _____

_____

_____

Now choose one site:

1. _____

_____

Why have you chosen this site over other sites? List your reasons here:

_____

_____

Plan what you really want out of this site.

_____

_____

In six month's time, you will have to decide if you want to continue using this site and revise your plan if you continue to use the site.

Reasons you would put your artwork on a third party website.

1. Publicity is good. The more you are 'out there' the better. You want people to see your work.

2. Visibility. These sites have a lot of followers. You will be seen by more people. This might lead them to your own website.

3. You are being found by people who love art. They will appreciate the quality of your work.

4. These sites are usually inexpensive and have easy to follow guidelines.

5. You do not have to upkeep the site yourself.

6. Some sites have 'print-on-demand' and this adds another special feature to your work. If people cannot afford an original, they can get a less expensive copy. You will receive a percentage of that sale....every time there is a sale

Negatives of joining a third party website.

1. You will need to pay a subscription fee or a percentage of the price of your artwork or both.

2. You have no control on how the work is marketed.

3. You cannot collect the emails of the clients you get through that site. The people that purchase your work are clients of the 3nd party website and not you (technically).

4. You are limited to the features that this site offers. You cannot add any features that you

may like or add any additional information than what is specified on the site.

5. If the site closes down, you will not have a site any more.

Ideas for selling reproductions

1. *Limited or open edition prints (framed or unframed) or canvas*

2. *Digital downloads–desktop wallpaper, stock photos, inspirational quote prints, etc.*

3. *Custom/commissions–original works in traditional or digital mediums*

4. *Merchandise–hats, mugs, t-shirts, enamel pins, etc.*

5. *Repeat prints on fabric or paper*

6. *Licensing work to other e-commerce merchants*

7. *Collaborations with merchants and creators*

NEW or RECENT Addition to other ways of selling your work is:

Auction Sales

Art auctions are a recent and very popular way to sell artwork. These auctions are online. There is a limited time to view and bid on the artwork, creating a sense of urgency. This can work in your favour. You may get a sale faster this way. You will get art lovers and people that frequently buy art. The provider of the art auction takes a percentage of the final price. This is often a percentage. That can be set by the provider or occasionally, negotiated.

However, the negative, is that you may not get the ideal price for your work. There is often a minimum bid that is set by the seller (you). You need to remember that if you get the minimum bid, the provider gets a percentage of that price. Figure out what the final price of the minimum bid is and make sure that is enough for you.

CHAPTER 14

PRICING YOUR WORK

Pricing your first piece of art, or even your 100th piece, can be extremely challenging.
Set the price too low and you could leave money on the table (you have sales but...), set the price too high and your artwork could start stacking up in your studio.

Thoughts XX By Doris Charest

How do you find that middle ground, that sweet spot? I've compiled four important do's and don'ts for pricing your art to help ensure your work finds a deserving home, and you get the salary you deserve!

DO: Research the Prices of Comparable Artists

How much do similar artists charge for their work? Thoroughly researching your market will give you a better idea of how to price your art. Consider other artists' work that is comparable in style, medium, colour, size, etc. Also look at those artists' accomplishments, experience, geographic location, and production rate.

Then search online, or visit galleries and open studios and see their art in person. Learn what those artists charge and why - as well as what price sells and what doesn't. This information can be an excellent gauge to help ensure your pricing is in the right ballpark.

DON'T: Undersell Your Work or Yourself

Creating art is time consuming and many of the materials you use can be expensive. Think about a reasonable hourly wage and the cost of materials when pricing your art - that includes framing and shipping, if applicable. Your price should reflect the money and time you put into creating your art.

Art biz whiz, Cory Huff of The Abundant Artist, uses this trick: "if my prices don't make me feel at least a little uncomfortable that I'm charging too much, I'm probably undercharging!" Charge what you're worth.

DO: Keep the Same Price For Your Studio and Galleries

If you're thinking of selling work from your studio at lower prices than your gallery, think again.

Galleries put time and energy into their sales and generally aren't happy to learn you've been selling work for a lot less. Take it from Art Biz Coach Alyson Stanfield, "They will drop you like a hot frying pan."

What's more, other galleries could learn about this and be less inclined to work with you. Make sure you have set prices that are generally the same for your studio and your galleries. That way people can buy your beautiful work from either place, and you can maintain a positive relationship with your galleries.

DON'T: Let Emotions Get in the Way

This is tough,. With all the time, creative effort and emotion you invest in your work, it's easy to get attached. Being proud of your work is wonderful, but letting emotion impact your pricing is not. Pricing your work needs to be predominantly based on its physical attributes and not on personal value. Emotional attachment are hard to explain to buyers. If there's a piece or two that are especially meaningful to you, consider keeping that work off the market and in your private collection.

DO: Have Confidence and Stand By Your Price

Whether you sell a lot of work or are new to the space, have confidence in yourself and your prices. If you don't, buyers will figure it out quickly. State your price firmly and let the buyer respond—and ignore any nagging inner thoughts about lowering it. When you take the time to properly and realistically price your work, you can stand behind the price. If the buyer wants to go below that, you'll be ready to justify your price. Confidence does wonders and will help you come home with the money you deserve.

Whether you're a new artist or switching mediums, determining a fair price for your art can pose a challenge. One would think that, after spending days, weeks, or months on a piece, an artist would know their work's value. However, countless artists find themselves unsure what to charge. Creativity, beauty, and a work's personal value are difficult to quantify, and the art industry's constantly, changing trends often influence a work's value as well.

Pricing your artwork fairly and consistently will make you appear more credible and reliable. Fair pricing will also give buyers reasonable expectations for purchasing or commissioning your work, which will likely help you increase sales and commissioned pieces.

Research Competitors

Researching your competition is a necessary part of the pricing process. Search popular, art-based websites for the sale prices and hourly rates of artists similar to you. The buyers who search for the work of these artists will likely see your work as well, so your pricing will need to appear comparable. Otherwise, these buyers will likely consider you overpriced or underpriced.

When comparing yourself to other artists, consider your similarities in the following areas:

Aesthetic. Some aesthetics become more popular than others, and thereby increase the prices for those artworks.

Materials and Medium. If an artwork consumes more materials, then it may cost more. Additionally, the art market has valued some mediums above others, such as large sculptures over canvas, and canvas over paper.

Originality. Original works often receive greater notice, and therefore, likely sell for more than unoriginal works, such as reprints.

Quality of Art. Work of a higher quality generally sells for more than copies of artworks.

Reputation. Emerging artists tend to price lower than established artists.

Size of Work. Larger works generally have larger prices than smaller works.

Venue (e.g. Gallery, Digital Art Marketplace, Art Fair, etc.). Some venues will have higher price points than others. For instance, open studios often sell less expensive works than commercial galleries. Keep in mind also that artists may include a venue's fees or commissions in a sales price.

Review

Reflecting on these criteria will help you determine how far above or below you should price your work compared to other artists. For instance, you might charge more for your work than an artist who matches all of the above criteria but appears to work in a smaller size than you, as smaller sizes often consume fewer materials and less time. The more criteria you have in common with an artist, the more closely your prices and that artist's prices should match. Take notes on your work and the work and prices of these artists as you research.

Calculate Costs

Accurately track the price of your materials purchased for and used in your artwork's creation. If you have a thorough record of these materials, then include them in the sales price of your artwork. Likewise, if you're selling through an agent, gallery or digital marketplace that charges a commission, include that commission in your sales price. Including the cost of materials and commission in your sales price will, at least, allow you to break even when you sell the work.

If a client has commissioned your work, then make sure that you keep a thorough and accurate record of the time, in minutes, spent on their project. By maintaining a detailed and organized record, you will appear professional and lower the likelihood of mistakenly over- or under-charging a client.

You can also price your artwork per square inch. For example, you can start at a $1.00 per square inch then add 5% slowly. The goal is to be consistent. As you sell more, you can raise your prices.

You might offer services, such as shipping the work or faster completion, instead of lowering the price. You might also accept the buyer's goods or services as a complete or partial trade for your work, but this is not recommended. However, artists do this all the time, for example - dentistry in exchange for a painting.

Raise your prices if:

•You receive a significant award. Winning major prizes demonstrates your skill and expertise in your field. Winning such awards also improves your reputation. For both of these reasons, buyers will pay more for your work.

•You are in high-profile shows. High-profile shows similarly demonstrate your ability as an artist. Furthermore, the buyers at high-profile shows will generally spend more on artwork.

•You are selling out of current stock. Selling out of current stock means there's great demand for your work at its current price. Consider raising your prices to see if you can earn more from your current audience.

Some artists raise their prices in relation to the cost of living. Others raise their prices according to their costs. Everything depends on the market in your area.

What other artists in your area are getting for their work and this work is similar to yours, is a good place to start.

Write down what your plan for pricing is here:

_____

_____

_____

_____

_____

_____

_____

_____

_____

_____

_____

_____

_____

_____

_____

_____

_____

_____

_____

CHAPTER 15

BUDGET

Working within your business' budget is the hardest task of all. Here we are going to figure out how much you have to spend on your art business and how you are going to spend it.

We will assess your needs and your actual income. We will plan for growth.

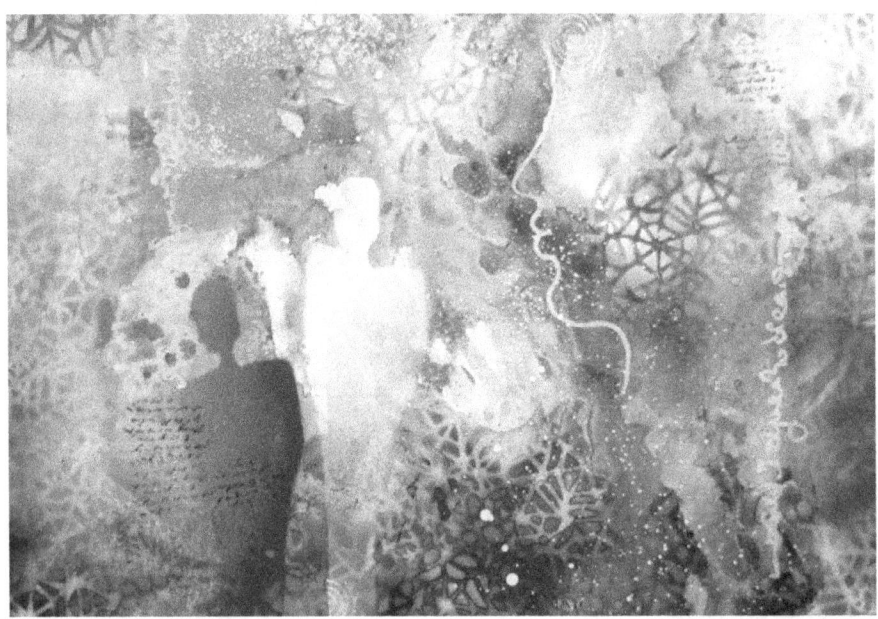

Thoughts IX by D. Charest

Track Your Spending and Revenue

First, you need to separate your personal spending and your business expenses. You should consider having separate credit cards and separate accounts for your business, it makes it easier to monitor.

Now, try to decide how much money do you need to keep your business going?

The best way to find this out is to track your spending on your business. Most artists do not really know how much they actually spend on their art in the beginning. You should track your spending on a monthly and yearly basis. To know how much you are really spending you should monitor your spending for 6 months (ideally).

You need to know how much money you are making and want to find ways to make the most of the money you have. You will need to track both your expenses and your revenue on a yearly basis in order to file your yearly personal income tax.

Once you know how much money you need for your art, you are ready.

Here's how it works:

STEP 1: MONEY IN List your sources of revenue for the last twelve months:

1._____

_____

_____

_____

_____

_____

2. _____

_____

_____

_____

_____

3. _____

_____

_____

_____

_____

4. _____

_____

_____

_____

_____

STEP 2: MONEY OUT

Next, look back over last 12 months of bank statements, credit card statements and cash receipts to help you list all of your associated expenses. This may take some time but it will give you a clear picture of where you are with expenses and this will make it easier for you to make a financial plan.

1._____

_____

_____

_____

_____

2._____

_____

_____

_____

_____

_____

3._____

_____

_____

_____

_____

_____

4._____

_____

_____

_____

_____

_____

STEP 3: ASSESS THE SITUATION.

Do you have enough revenue for your expenses?
Where are the big expenditures? Where is the big
revenue?

Make a plan. Do you want to raise the revenue?
How? do you want to lower the expenses? How?

_____

_____

_____

_____

_____

_____

_____

_____

_____

_____

_____

_____

_____

_____

_____

_____

_____

_____

STEP 4: Using and Maintaining Your Budget

Think about your financial goals for your art business.

Identify your short-term and long-term goals, and make saving for those goals part of your budget.

For example, goals may be:

- Buy 100 business cards

- Print 100 flyers about me and my artwork

- Pay for a website

- Pay for prints of my work

- Buy 10 canvases for my next series

- Hire someone to do social media for me

- Hire someone to do work on my website

- Buy better quality paint. This will double my costs but it will be worth it.

- Hire someone to create a publicity video that I can put on my site

- Have enough money to go to an 'artist in residence' course in another country or visit an exhibit at the National Gallery in November

List 5 goals here:

1._____

_____

_____

_____

_____

_____

2._____

_____

_____

3. _____

4. _____

5. _____

Basic financial advice given to most people also applies to your art business:

Know where your art money is going. Write down your expenses and keep your receipts.

Keep a copy of bills you pay during this time.

Divide your expenses into two categories: "needs" (for example, a new canvas) and "wants" (for example, a fancy new laptop to make your website).

Tracking your money will help you figure out your income and your expenses. Every dollar you spend has an impact on your overall budget.

Small changes to spending habits can have a big impact on your budget and your ability to save. Ask yourself if you really need that new brush. Can you save the money and put it towards your business cards or advertising?

Needs and wants aren't the same for everyone. A need could be a gallon of red paint for one person (a muralist) but a single tube is a need for a miniaturist.

Your needs and wants may also change over time. For example, you may need only a small studio now but in five years you may need a larger space.

This will help you understand your spending habits. If you need to reduce your spending, your "wants" may be an area to target.

When making a budget ask yourself:

•Are there any small recurring expenses that you can cut?

•Are there expenses in the "wants" categories that you can cut?

•Do you want to add money to new savings categories that reflect your financial goals? For example, saving for a trip to see galleries in New York.

•Are you limiting your spending (as much as possible) to what is in your budget?

•Are you keeping receipts and bills?

•Are you listing your revenue and expenses?

•Are you comparing your budget to what you actually spend at the end of each month and year?

•Are there big or small differences between your actual spending and your budget?

•Which categories have the largest differences?

•Are the differences because of an unusual situation or is this likely to happen each month?

- Are you able to save enough money to reach your financial goals   and are you able to set spending limits?

- Can you reduce costs?

- Can you find more money for your art expenses?

Tips to help you make a budget

Continue with the previous exercise each month, many people make this a regular habit at the end of each month.

If you're actual spending varies only a little from your budget, you're on the right track.

Every personal budget needs to have a purpose, otherwise, what's the point of doing all this work?

Decide what your purpose is. Is your budget enough to cover expenses? Making enough for a trip to see the treasures of the Louvre? Is it taking a course by your favourite artist? Is it selling enough artwork to go to an art expo in Europe? Is it selling scarves with your paintings on it so that you can get noticed by fashion designers? Your goals can be the stuff of dreams. You are allowed to dream.

Your main interest is in finding out how much money you do have and where you want to spend it. Once you know that, you can work towards this goal. The good news is that by simply creating a monthly budget, you can open up more opportunities to increase savings because you will be able to identify the areas in your spending that you can cut back.

The way you track your expenses can vary, depending on the advice you get. Below is a very basic model you can use to start with. Remember that there are many ways to do your accounting and you need to choose the way that is best for you. My way may not work for you.

Excel is one of the best programs you can use to make a budget. It is relatively easy to use and you can make your own spreadsheets.

To track your basic expenses, you can set up your spreadsheet like this (this is only an example):

	January	February	March
Revenue			
Art revenue			
Card revenue			
Online revenue			
Teaching income			

Workshop income

Expenses

Artist fees for entering shows

Blue Beauties   By Doris Charest

Flyers

Website cost

Advertising and postage

Art supplies

CHAPTER 16

TAXES

Taxes need to be paid if you sell any work, this is the law. This section will give you broad categories that you can use for starting your record keeping.

What you can do is collect the information about how much it cost you to produce the artwork, how much it cost you to make it ready to show and how much it cost you to travel the work back and forth to that art show.

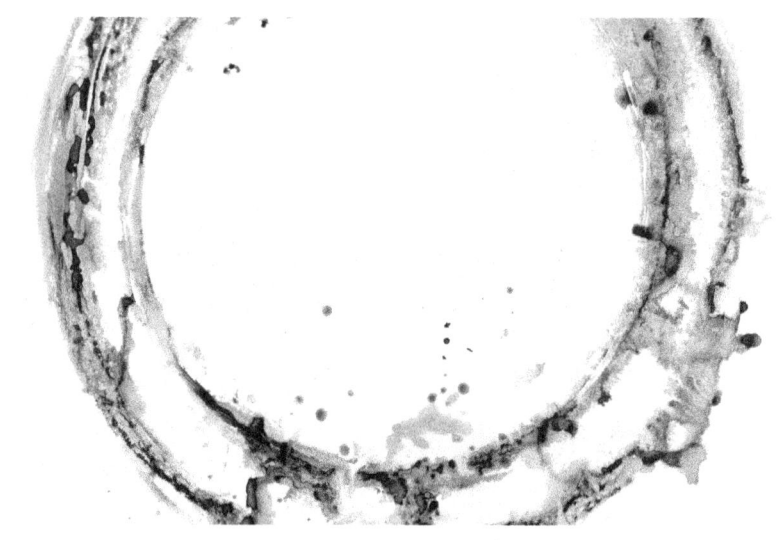

Circle of life   By Doris Charest

Expenses

My first bit of advice is to talk to an expert (your accountant) about small art businesses. Ask about tax rules in your area.

Rules for taxes differ depending on the province, state or country in which you live. In this chapter, I present what is possible where I live (Alberta, Canada). Find out what is possible where you live.

Remember: all income must be reported!

First of all, you need to list all sources of revenue related to art. Make sure you clarify with your accountant how the revenue must be recorded on your business income statement and your yearly income tax filing.

List your revenue from your:

-teaching income (if you teach art classes)

-workshop income

-rental of your art

- consulting, this can include being a juror for an art show or giving a talk to an art group

-sales of images of one of your artworks to make cards or wallpaper (as an example)

-tutoring in art

-sales of cups with your design on them

-sales of prints with your images on it

Make a list of all your sources of revenue. You may have one source or 10. List what you have.

1._____

_____

_____

2._____

_____

_____

_____

_____

3._____

_____

_____

_____

_____

4._____

_____

_____

_____

_____

5._____

_____

_____

_____

_____

6._____

_____

_____

_____

_____

7._____

_____

_____

_____

_____

8._____

_____

_____

_____

_____

Expenses

Now for the expenses. Again, check what the rules in your area, but these are some of the possible deductions where I live:

Art materials of any kind with receipts

Travel to purchase those art materials, but to be able to deduct mileage, you need to keep a mileage log in your car. I talk about this later.

Administrative costs like postage, paper for photocopies, ink for the copier etc... if you use that copier only for your art business. If you share the family copier, then figure out what percentage of the family photocopier paper and ink go towards your business and that is what you deduct. Postage paid for sending out applications or proposals is deductible as are the envelopes.

Travel to deliver or pick-up artwork, to go your show's opening or another artist's opening, to pick up art supplies, to deliver a proposal, to deliver a proposal or any other travel related to your work is deductible. You need to keep a mileage log for your car showing the kilometres you drove to the art activity and back from the art activity to your home. If you do, then you can deduct all your mileage related to your art business. Check with your accountant for your area.

For a studio outside the home, all rental costs can be deducted.

I you have an art studio in your home, measure your square footage used by your studio, what % of your whole home square footage that is used by your art activities and you can deduct that % of the mortgage or rent, % of heating, water, sewer, electrical, the home phone, insurance and property taxes.

You can use the 10% (for example) that you use if your home space and deduct that % of the taxes also.

Consider how much of your phone you use for business. If you use your phone for 20% of the time (for example) for your art business, you can deduct 20% of the fixed expenses of your phone.

If you use your computer just for your art business, you can deduct all the computer depreciation. If you use your computer 50% of the time for your art business, then you can deduct 50% of the depreciation expenses.

In my area, meals out for business are not deductible. In some locations, they are.

List some possible expenses here related to your business. After you have made the list, contact your accountant to decide what information will be used for those deductions for both the Art Income Statement and Income Tax reporting.

1._____

_____

_____

2._____

_____

_____

3. _____

_____

_____

_____

_____

4. _____

_____

_____

_____

_____

5. _____

_____

_____

_____

_____

6. _____

_____

_____

_____

_____

7._____

_____

_____

_____

_____

8._____

_____

_____

_____

_____

My best advice is to consult a local accountant that is familiar with small businesses and art businesses if you can. Keep good records and you will most likely not have any problems. Honesty is the best policy.

Look up accountants, ask for references from other artists for accountants and list them here:

1._____

_____

_____

_____

_____

2._____

_____

_____

_____

_____

3._____

_____

_____

_____

_____

4._____

_____

_____

You can interview accountants to see if they would meet your needs. A short phone conversation is a good start. List here what you would ask them. For example, you could ask why they have chosen to work with small businesses. What are the reasons they like small businesses? What can they do for you that other accountants cannot?

1._____

_____

_____

_____

_____

2._____

_____

_____

_____

_____

3._____

_____

_____

_____

_____

4. _____

_____

_____

_____

_____

5. _____

_____

_____

_____

_____

6. _____

_____

_____

_____

_____

7. _____

_____

_____

_____

_____

Finding an accountant that you are compatible
with and feel easy asking questions to is important.

CHAPTER 17

SCAMS

Be careful! Be Professional! This the best advice.
Here are stories of people who got scammed. Scammers will come up with even better ways than the ones mentioned here so just be aware that it is a possibility.

Being aware and be professional

Buying on instalments

Some people love art and cannot manage to save money to buy it so they ask to pay in two or three different payments. You can do this if you choose. It is a good way to sell art if you are careful. There are options:

1. You take their post dated cheques and give them the artwork. You will need to be sure that your client will not keep the work and put a stop payment on the cheques. This has happened to a friend of mine. The client stopped paying. Most people are, however, are honest.

2. You take cash on the first of every month until the work is paid. Give the client a receipt every time with a note on the receipt showing how much they have paid so far and how much is left. This will encourage them to continue.

3. Be more professional. Provide bills of sale. Provide receipts. Write everything down. You can set up any kind of plan you want but be sure that the person will pay.

Be aware that part of being a _professional_ artist is learning business procedures. Take a class or ask someone you know to teach you the basics.

Internet scams

As soon as you have a website, you will start to have 'scammers'.

Steps to check on the Scammers.

1. Some scammers will say 'I am from XX, NZ and I want your artwork for a present for my husband or wife. Can you send the work right away? My check is in the mail. Do NOT send any artwork until the cash is in your hand. If you get a cheque, make sure that you can cash it and you are sure that the money is in your account. Wait the right amount of business days for the cheque to clear.

I had someone send me a cheque. That was good. That is a first step. I took it to the bank. My bank would not honour the cheque. They said they could not verify that it was a 'real' cheque and sent me to the bank that it was drawn on. (This took two hours)

 I went to that bank. They tried to verify this cheque. They could not link the cheque to any bank account. They told me this was a fake cheque and sent me to the fraud department of the local police. They investigated.

If I had just deposited the cheque, the money would have showed up in my bank account but later it would have been removed when they realized that this was an invalid cheque. I would have sent the work and I would have lost both the money and the artwork.   Lesson: Alway check with the bank.

Later, I was told that if I had deposited the cheque, the scammers would have had access to my bank account. There are stories of the scammers using the artists' bank account information so they could use your identity to get credit cards, get a loan or more. This is a form of identity theft.

2. Another scam is that the purchasers all of a sudden need help with the border tax or shipping. Therefore, they ask for you to pay this expense and then they will refund the money. My friend, trusting artist he was, paid this expense and waited for the refund. No refund ever came.

There are new ways to scam every day. This is only a few of the ideas that I have some across.

Here are some ways to avoid these issues.

1. If you have a gallery, sell the work through the gallery. They have insurance if the sale is not real.

2. If you sell online, some sites verify for you. I sold one piece on Ebay when I was testing to see if Ebay was a good place to sell art. I was new to selling then and I needed help with the transaction. I called Ebay and they found that the

sale was a scam. I was ready to send the work because I expected this site to have already verified but they told me that I should never send the work until the cash is in my account.

3. Online galleries usually verify the sales of artwork. I have sold work through sites and there were so many steps to the sale that I got frustrated. However, I was told that was their way of verifying. Their system worked. I now believe in the multistep system.

If you have a feeling that the sale is not right, stop and verify. Don't be shy about this step. Verifying is part of the process of becoming a professional.

HAVING YOUR WORK HANG IN A BUSINESS FOR PUBLICITY

Some businesses ask artists if they would like to hang their artwork in their business as a way to get their work seen by a different audience. This is not quite a scam but it can be. Some businesses actively promote the artist and their work. However, some businesses do not. They just use the work to decorate their premises. Check out the business first.

Some businesses offer a small rental fee for the work.

Most businesses do not take any commission for the work since you are decorating their premises for free.

If you say yes to putting your work up at a business:

Make sure you have contract with the business. Indicate the works that showing, the size, the price and even a photo if you can. Indicate how long the work will be at the business. Indicate how you are going to get paid if there is a sale. Write down any details.

Check regularly (drop in) after the work is up. Make sure your business cards are available and the labels on your paintings are visible and up. Sometimes, labels disappear (accidentally). If the labels disappear often, reconsider having your work in that business.

CHAPTER 19

CONCLUSION

Thank-you for taking my course 'Starting an art business'. I hope that I have given you enough information to get you started in the right direction.

Here are some parting thoughts that I want to share:

Art photo by D. Charest

Parting Advice

This book is about the journey more than the goal.

Here are some basic principles to keep in mind:

1. You will have to work hard.

2. You will develop good working habits. You will be doing what you love along with some serious planning.

3. You will need to keep rooted in knowing that you will succeed one small step at a time. The best flow comes with fun and joy.

4. Master the hard skills first.

5. You will need to plan long uninterrupted stretches of time. Working 'in the flow' means you get more done in less time.

6. Work on removing distractions and working with purpose (flow).

7. Use downtime to think about your work and plan.

8. Create mini-deadlines to help you finish work, finishing should be a habit. Many artists tend to start and not finish, you need to practice finishing.

9. Practice quitting bad ideas.

10. Give up perfectionism; take up doing your best within certain parameters.

11. "Opportunity is missed by most people because it is dressed in overalls and looks like work." (Thomas Edison)

12. "Don't quit before the miracle happens." (Fannie Flagg) I like this last piece of advice. Persistence is important.

13. In Canada, there is an association called CARFAC. They are the national voice of Canada's professional visual artists. As a non-profit association and a National Art Service Organization, their mandate is to promote the visual arts in Canada. They are a great source of information regarding contracts, fees, and legal issues. Here is their web site:https://www.carfac.ca/about/

Web sites for you to check out and Websites that I used for references:

Web sites for you to check out and Websites that I used for references:

https://www.format.com/magazine/resources/art/how-to-promote-your-art

https://www.lifewire.com/what-exactly-is-twitter-2483331

https://blog.dashburst.com/best-sites-to-buy-sell-art/

https://www.digitalunite.com/technology-guides/tv-video/youtube/what-youtube

https://www.canada.ca/en/financial-consumer-agency/services/make-budget.html

https://www.creditcanada.com/how-to-create-a-monthly-budget

https://www.lifewire.com/what-exactly-is-twitter-2483331

https://artplusmarketing.com/the-15-best-websites-to-sell-art-online-b0ea6fd8ffd5

https://www.format.com/magazine/resources/art/how-to-promote-your-art

https://www.lifewire.com/what-exactly-is-twitter-2483331

https://blog.dashburst.com/best-sites-to-buy-sell-art/

https://www.digitalunite.com/technology-guides/tv-video/youtube/what-youtube

https://www.canada.ca/en/financial-consumer-agency/services/make-budget.html

https://www.creditcanada.com/how-to-create-a-monthly-budget

https://www.lifewire.com/what-exactly-is-twitter-2483331

https://artplusmarketing.com/the-15-best-websites-to-sell-art-online-b0ea6fd8ffd5

Wikipedia

https://www.carfac.ca/about/

ABOUT THE ARTIST

Artist in her studio

I started art as a hobby. My husband was transferred to Texas and as a Canadian, I could not work or go to university. I was at a loss of what to do with myself. My neighbour took me with her to her painting class, where I fell in love with painting, and the rest is history. My hobby grew all while raising children and working, until it became my full-time work.

My passion for painting has never stopped. I've taken classes in Texas, Arizona, Quebec and Alberta. My attraction to texture and colour is due to my growing up on a farm in northern Alberta where fields of wheat, canola and flax provided colours for my palette even then. They are the fuel for the memories I use for my paintings.

Mixed media is my favourite form of painting. I love the variety of media because it helps tell stories. When creating a painting, I have a story in mind but I also wants the viewer to create their own story or relationship with the painting and evoke memories for them.

Nature is my main inspirations. Capturing memories of my experiences in a way that a camera cannot, my paintings invite you to explore the subject; quietly discovering what is really there.

dorischarest@gmail.com

Doris' website: www.dorischarest.ca

I have creativity courses and art courses online at: https://www.udemy.com/user/dorischarest/

For more information on mixed media by Doris Charest:

https://www.youtube.com/channel/UCltBfqSMAKoOOWeXaKGud6Q?view_as=subscriber

https://www.facebook.com/dorischarest

https://www.pinterest.ca/dalinec/

https://www.instagram.com/dorischarest/

https://www.udemy.com/user/edit-profile/

https://www.skillshare.com/user/dorischarest

All photography and artwork by Doris Charest

Thanks for reading. Till next time ...

Doris Charest